Life Skills for Teens and Tweens (2 Books in 1)

How to Cook, Manage Money, Solve Problems, Develop Social Skills, and More

Important Skills Kids Need but Don't Learn in School

The Mentor Bucket

Table of Contents

Book - 1
Life Skills for Teens Workbook

Book - 2
Life Skills for Tweens Workbook

Book – 1

Life Skills for Teens Workbook

35+ Essentials for Winning in the Real World

How to Cook, Manage Money, Drive a Car, and Develop Manners, Social Skills, and More

INTRODUCTION

Hey buddy!

Welcome to your teenage years.

The years ahead will be an exciting yet ever-changing period of your life. But the question is, how prepared are you for the next phase of your life? Can you confidently do things independently without calling on your parents at every slight chance?

The teenage years come with excitement and challenges, and it is usually the age to prepare and start getting ready to live independently. This is a time to gather the bricks and materials you need to start building and transition into adulthood. In addition, you'll soon start making important decisions that set the pace for your future.

When you make those mindful decisions, you can start transforming each experience into a great opportunity for learning. And the experiences, furthermore, help you become a more mature and responsible teenager.

So, I ask again — How prepared are you for what lies ahead?

Have you prepared for a successful adult life where you'll achieve your dreams and live on your terms? Do you have enough life skills to succeed in the real world?

If you answered "No" to any of these questions, it's okay. Don't be too hard on yourself or feel inadequate. After all, we were all born as blank slates and had to learn everything we do; we weren't born knowing how to sit, crawl, walk, talk, and dance. All these were learned skills. Likewise, you can learn other skills to help you get by in this demanding world.

Today, getting good grades and schooling isn't enough to get by; you need life skills as your anchor. School teaches history, facts and numbers, writing and reading skills, math, and rudimentary sciences. However, you need more than these to function properly in your daily life. Don't get me wrong; I'm not suggesting that schooling is unimportant. Of course, it is! But there is more to life than what's taught in the classroom.

While your focus may be on getting into the top college and graduating high school with flying colors, you might tend to overlook an important aspect — developing skills that can last you a lifetime.

We are all born with responsibilities that we can't escape. So, it's better to accept them wholeheartedly and prepare by learning life skills rather than complaining. Especially if you want to enjoy your adulthood.

Adulthood comes with many wonders and challenges. From managing a bank account to paying taxes, there's just so much you need to know. I bet you've heard stories of teens who go off to college and never make a meal for themselves or do their laundry; they don't know what to do in emergencies or know what leadership entails.

I can still remember my first year at college. Every day, I was living off takeout because that was the only thing I knew how to make. It took me no time to go from being unhealthy to looking like the "dreaded Freshman." Within a few weeks, I got to my highest weight ever! Sadly, my waistline wasn't the only thing that added in size. My credit card and student loan debt skyrocketed. Who would've thought managing money and spending it wouldn't be a piece of cake?

I didn't know I would be forced to step up to be responsible by scheduling my doctor's appointments, preparing meals for myself, making important decisions, being self-reliant, eating healthy, keeping fit, learning how to cope with my emotions, and so much more. I didn't know that words like taxes, rates, and late fees mean much, so I acted ignorantly and had to learn the hard way — incurring debt! I didn't know much about communication skills, empathy, and active listening. Wow, I didn't know a lot of things!

It took a lot of exploring, reading, learning, and practicing to help me better navigate and reposition myself. But even though I had to go through the tough route, you don't have to. Looking back now, I realize all I missed out on. My life would've been much easier with the knowledge I have now. I don't want you to have the same regrets as I did when you get older, and that has been my motivation for teaching life skills to teens for over five years now.

Of course, you can pick up some of these skills on your own. But wouldn't you rather give yourself a leg up by preparing now instead of waiting?

These life skills are more than what you'll learn in your four-year experience in high school. They are skills that will prepare you to become a productive member of society — independent, dependable, responsible, and someone who knows how to survive and thrive independently. Of course, high school helps you develop some of these essential skills. However, it is mostly not enough to mold you into a successful adult; you need to learn more if you want to spearhead your successful future.

As you grow older, you're taking on more responsibilities. You've probably wondered how your mom and dad could do some adult tasks and make them seem like a breeze. As you grow, learn, and experience new things, the urge to be well-rounded in basic skills will increase.

Thankfully, you have this book to support you and serve as your go-to guide for solving daily teen and adult problems that you've been shying away from and taking for granted.

I've seen many teens shy away from self-independence and pin their freedom on the "No route" — no happiness, no growth, and no success. However, they quickly forget that their emotional, financial, personal, and professional values have their foundation in self-independence.

By building yourself for independence, you will gain a sense of happiness that's not easy to come by; one that you can't get just anywhere. You will build a bigger perspective of life and increase your awareness and knowledge. You will learn to manage your emotions and have better relationships with people, boosting your self-confidence and self-worth. Now, more than ever, your reputation affects your growth and how you've advanced in your career. Your independence will help create a strong reputation for you.

I am writing this book to help you stand on your feet. It will empower you with the right tools and mindset to balance the crucial aspects of your life. I have developed this book with my personal experience of being a teenager who has struggled with and conquered dependency, as well as picked up the many skills I've acquired and the knowledge I've gained from the life experiences of teenagers I've worked with.

Even though the internet offers a wealth of knowledge, it can be overwhelming to navigate through it and narrow it down to what's helpful to you. It can also be tedious trying to figure out what's accurate and what isn't. Also, while you can ask your parents or trusted relatives to teach you specific skills, you may miss out on other essential skills they aren't familiar with. However, this book gives you a complete guide that will help you build a strong foundation for the future you've always admired and wished for.

One of the greatest gifts any parent can give their child is to prepare them for the future by teaching them invaluable life skills. So, if you're a parent who gifted this book to your teen, I must commend you for taking this crucial step and wanting the best for your teen.

As the name suggests, this book will teach you 35+ life skills that will make your adulthood easier! It will offer you the information you'll need to maximize your potential and live a fun-filled life.

I can promise you that you should be well equipped and ready to take on anything by the time you've finished reading this book.

So, whether you're still in school, just finishing school, heading off to college, or you've already found yourself in the real world, it's never too late to learn essential skills that will make you win in the real world.

Let's get started!

CHAPTER 1
INTRODUCTION TO LIFE SKILLS

Growing up is something you can never be too prepared for since life won't pause for you while you get ready. The world will keep moving with or without you. Moreover, nature has dictated that you must grow older as the clock ticks; therefore, you're bound to experience many internal and external changes.

At some point, you'll be spurred to take charge and prepare for independence. You'll then gradually start handling responsibilities while balancing the rapid changes you're experiencing. The choices you make at this age will strongly impact your future.

During my teenage years, it was challenging to handle all the changes I experienced. I wished there was a magic wand I could use to make everything easier then. Even though I wasn't lucky enough to get the magic wand I wanted, I will ensure you get yours through this book. This book is your magic wand. I have written it using my experiences as a teen and those of highly skilled and experienced people. It will teach you all the life skills you need to know to navigate this challenging world without getting overwhelmed.

But first, what exactly is a life skill?

What Is a Life Skill?

The United Nations International Children's Emergency Fund (UNICEF) defined life skills as *"psycho-social abilities for adaptive and positive behavior that enable individuals to deal effectively with the demands and challenges of everyday life."* Likewise, the World Health Organization defines life skills as *"the abilities for adaptive and positive behavior that enable individuals to deal effectively with the demands and challenges of everyday life."*

Life skills help you adapt and cope with the daily challenges life may throw your way. Close your eyes for a few seconds and imagine how you live your daily life. Do you notice there are certain things you repeat every day? It could be relaxing with your parents, tidying up your room, watching TV with your siblings, or even dropping a dollar bill into your piggy bank. Do you know that it's life skills that help you get by and carry out these tasks effectively? You can think of life skills as qualities you need to function effectively as a teen. Any skill that positively impacts your life can be categorized as a life skill.

Life skills are qualities that help you handle the pressures of daily life. They encompass the behaviors you engage in to be independent and successful in your daily life. Without life skills, you may struggle with making healthy choices and meeting your daily needs.

As you get yourself prepared for independence, it's essential that you learn valuable skills to help you solve problems, make informed decisions, communicate effectively, think critically and effectively, build healthy relationships, manage your emotions, empathize with others, and manage yourself healthily and productively. These skills are needed so you can become the best version of yourself.

Why Life Skills?

The teenage years should be a time for building the foundation for your future. This is the time for personal development and preparing for the challenges ahead. During this time, you will face challenges that will test your patience. So how do you manage without getting into any trouble? By learning life skills!

Life skills will teach you how to solve the various challenges you'll face in your everyday life. In addition, they will teach you how to navigate the world without parental supervision.

Teens with a life skills education know their abilities and what they are expected to do. They know their strengths and their limits and can set healthy boundaries. They are smart enough to know how to make things easier for themselves and others.

Who Needs Life Skills?

Everyone does! Your dad, mum, friends from next door, teachers, and even classmates from school. Every human needs specific life skills to help them function and be more effective. As a teen, you need to develop life skills more than ever because you're in a transient stage, and you'll need them to get by.

Different Challenges Teens Encounter

Your experience during your teenage years will mold your general beliefs and ideologies in life. As a result, overcoming the obstacles you'll face is usually challenging. But with life skills, the journey should be easier and more enjoyable.

A few decades ago, teens' common challenges were starting a family and choosing a career path. Today, we see teens facing problems that are peculiar to them. The following are challenges you may be facing as a teen:

Acceptance

It is normal to feel awkward in a new environment. Everyone finds it challenging to blend into situations when out of their comfort zone. As a teen, you will find it even more difficult to sense rejection. For example, if you are new to the baseball team in your school, you may not be as welcomed as you've hoped because the team members are just meeting you. However, you don't need to force yourself to be accepted, and you don't need to feel bad as long as you have the right skills to handle such awkward situations.

Sexuality

You may think it strange that everyone is experimenting with sex, and you feel left out. You wonder if your sex hormones are working or if your friends will laugh at you for not experimenting with sex. You don't need to be bothered about these things. Your sexual hormones are very active at this point in your life, so it is normal to feel the way you do. Know that nobody can force or compel you to do anything you don't want to.

Managing Stress

Growing up comes with its responsibilities. You'll have more domestic duties to take care of at home. In addition, your assignments will get more challenging at school and take longer than they usually do. These developments can be stressful for most teens since they are stepping into bigger shoes than they've ever tried on before. They'll need to work harder to fill up those shoes.

Issues with Siblings

Your siblings love you but may not understand that you have evolved and have more responsibilities. This could lead to conflict between you. For example, in the past, it was okay for both of you to play in your room, leaving it messy because mom would always come and tidy it up. However, that may not be the case any longer because you are expected to do certain things for yourself, which may cause issues between you and your sibling.

Perhaps you used to play football with your brother every day, but you can no longer do that because of your commitments — homework, house chores, and school projects. Your relationship with your sibling could become strained because of these.

Academic Problems

Academics constitute a significant part of a teen's life; having difficulties in other areas of life can manifest in academics. Teens may experience poor academic performance, fear of going to school, dropping out, and absenteeism.

Balancing school challenges can be a bit of a trial for you. Unfortunately, because of this, your schoolwork might start to suffer, affecting your grades. Therefore, taking things slowly is best to avoid putting undue pressure on yourself.

Peer Pressure

This is undoubtedly the most significant challenge teens face. When all your friends are doing something you do not want to do, it may be difficult for you to remain true to yourself; this leaves you struggling with your emotions. For example, when your friends are out attending a party, and you aren't there, you will feel left out, right? That's what peer pressure does; it makes you feel alone and that you should join others in what they do, good or bad.

Social Media

Social media is a vast space where you interact with various people with different backgrounds and opinions. However, if you give in to social media pressure, you might lose your "self."

Social media can expose you to many risks, including fraud, cyberbullying, offensive images, rumor spreading, and unrealistic views of others and the world. This can cause anxiety and depression, unrealistic expectations, stress, negative body image, unhealthy sleep patterns, and addiction.

Benefits of Life Skills

When teenagers are taught life skills, they learn abilities that will help them solve problems, make good decisions, and communicate effectively. In addition, teaching teens life skills encourages positive behavior.

Teens with the proper life skills can develop empathy and foster healthy relationships for themselves and those around them. With life skills, teens can be empowered to take charge of their lives.

CHAPTER 2
UNIVERSAL SKILLS

If you want to succeed at anything, then you need universal skills! Universal skills are generally accepted and valued all over the world. Universal skills help us to cope in whatever situation or environment we find ourselves in. It lets us relate well with others and live our best lives even in new places.

Let us assume that I take a fish away from its home in the Atlantic Ocean and throw it into the Pacific Ocean. This fish will survive in the water. This is because it has a universal skill that is common to all kinds of fishes — it can swim. So, it doesn't matter whether the fish is in a stream or pond, it will still survive. This is precisely how it is for human beings too.

Regardless of race or status, we all have the same universal skills. If you leave your home country for another country for a holiday, the universal skills are still the same. It is not like culture, which changes from place to place.

Universal skills are helpful in many aspects of life. They prepare you to face real-life challenges. Being the person with the highest grade in your class isn't enough. What matters is how well you handle the tasks left in your care. With universal skills, you will be self-sufficient and know how to survive on your own.

The following are skills you should master to succeed in different areas of your life:

Leadership

To understand leadership, first, you need to know what it is not.

Leadership isn't what you should leave to the captain of your football team. It doesn't entail throwing commands at people and forcing them to do your bidding. Leadership isn't about being in the spotlight and taking all the credit. A leader is not someone that forces their opinions on their friends. They don't claim to know it all and don't make everything about themselves.

Leadership starts from the little things you do every day.

Do you mistreat your younger siblings? Do you ignore your mum when she tells you to do something? Are your friends scared of the things you do when you are angry? Do you carry out the tasks assigned to you? Do you just suck up your feelings and feel spiteful when offended?

If you answered "yes" to any of these questions, you probably aren't doing a great job of leading the people around you. Being a good leader means putting your desires aside and listening to the concerns and suggestions of others. It means making decisions that will be in everyone's interest.

How to Be a Good Leader

The following are steps you should take to be a good leader:

Lead by example

When you lead by example, you guide others through your behavior; showing rather than telling. The aim is to inspire people around you to copy your behavior. You shouldn't say one thing and do something else. It should be more like *"Do as I do"* and not *"Do as I say."* For example, do not tell your sibling to keep their hands off the wall if you wouldn't go by that rule too.

The people around you will likely follow in your footsteps when you prove yourself. Yelling orders at people never really works. If you want them to get a particular task done, show them how. Do it first!

Be a good listener

Being a good listener means thoughtfully and comprehensively focusing on what another person is saying and engaging in their ideas. It isn't all about hearing what the person says — it entails committing to digesting the information presented and responding constructively.

To be a good leader, you have to first acknowledge that you can't know everything and be willing to listen to others. To be a good listener, pay attention to the speaker, show that you are listening, provide feedback, defer judgment, and respond appropriately.

Be patient

Leadership isn't easy-peasy. You will need lots of patience to sail through, especially during a crisis. You will need to retain composure in the face of adversity to ensure others remain calm. When others around you show signs of strain, don't get irritated. Support them instead.

Everyone has opinions and beliefs that may be different from yours. Regardless, be patient with them and listen to their views.

Communicate effectively

Effective communication is integral to being a good leader; you need this skill to succeed. Of course, communication can take different forms, but effectively navigating it allows you to relate better with others and be more fulfilled.

Leadership requires that you make people understand what you are doing and why you are doing it. One way to do that is to practice active listening and give your feedback afterward. You can start learning to be a good leader by cultivating small habits such as talking things through with your siblings instead of quarreling and listening to people's ideas and giving your suggestions.

Exercise for leadership skills

Write answers to the following questions.

How do you react when others disagree with your opinion?

_____

_____

_____

_____

_____

_____

How do you react when addressing large crowds?

_____

_____

_____

_____

_____

_____

_____

What would you do to improve your leadership skills?

_____

_____

_____

_____

_____

_____

_____

Goal Setting

Goal setting is the act of taking steps toward achieving your desired outcome. What is your dream? What do you plan to become? Maybe your dream is to be a musician, teacher, doctor, or therapist. Whatever your dream is, achieving it requires that you set goals. The goals will be broken down into smaller and more attainable steps that drive you toward success.

It is crucial that you set goals for yourself to avoid getting distracted along the way. When you set goals, you have something to look forward to. Additionally, this clarifies what to do and how to get it done. You won't do things because they feel good at that moment; you will consider the future gains and consequences.

Without goals, you will lose focus and direction. But *with* goals, you will be in the driver's seat; having the power to transform your life in whichever direction you want.

How to Set Goals

To accomplish your goals, you will need to plan them. This process involves considering different options, their risks and benefits, and the work required to achieve those goals. The following are steps to take to make the most out of your goal-setting process:

Picture the kind of person you want to be

What kind of person do you want to be when you are older? What do you want your family and friends to know you for? What would make you happy if you could do them? Your goal might be to get into college, join the Boy Scouts, or be the president of your school club. It all depends on what you want.

Try to imagine yourself in a few years. What do you see yourself doing? This will help you determine and know what you should work toward.

Set realistic goals

No doubt, all your goals are valid. However, some are not meant for you at that stage of your life.

What do you think of a fourteen-year-old who wants to buy a car and house before turning sixteen? I don't know about you, but I would laugh it off. Although I can't rule out the possibility, isn't that too much of a burden or too unrealistic?

It is better to set realistic goals so you won't end up disappointed at the end of the day.

Focus

As you've outlined your goals, stick to them and don't look back. Perhaps, your friends may have bigger goals than you, and you may feel left out. But, do not be deceived — everyone has their race to run. So, keep working on your goals, achieve them, and then go for bigger ones.

Do not become distracted by how attractive other people's goals are. Instead, work toward achieving what you want. What may work for your friends might be a terrible move for you. Concentrate on your goals and devise small but realistic plans to achieve them.

Do things that bring you closer to your goals

Do you sleep all day and skip practice hours when preparing for a big competition? Unless you are planning for failure, you'll take practice seriously. You will practice until you get better. The same applies to your goals.

If your goal is to read a book monthly, start by reading a page daily. If your goal is to save $300 by the end of the year, start by buying a piggy bank and saving 2 cents a day.

Ensure your actions lead you to your goal. Make little, daily steps to push yourself closer to where you want to be.

It's okay to change your goals

You are still young, trying to understand yourself and your potential, so your goals can change. If you feel your goals are not in line with your values and the person you're growing to be, change them.

Goals can be adjusted to meet your changing needs. If you are unsure, you can ask for help from your parents. They've been there before, so they will help you in whatever way they can.

Exercise for goal setting

Write answers to the following questions.

Imagine yourself in a few years. What do you want to be known for? This should include where you want to live, work, or study (if you plan to attend college).

_____

_____

_____

_____

_____

_____

What steps do you need to take to bring you closer to achieving your goals?

_____

_____

_____

_____

_____

_____

Intellectual Curiosity

Intellectual curiosity is how eager a person is to learn new things. If you are intellectually curious, learning new things will be a fun and natural process rather than a chore for you. You will be willing and desire to know more.

Intellectual curiosity raises you from simply passing tests and having good grades in school to being knowledgeable about the outside world.

When I was a teenager, I was inquisitive. I wanted to know how and why everything happened the way it did. I recall asking my dad why we had twelve months in a year rather than six or some other random number. He laughed about it, but I eventually got my answer. He gave me Julius Caesar's explanation, telling me about the need for 12 months and the additional leap year to synchronize with the seasons.

So, I am asking you, "What else do you know besides your schoolwork?" Educate yourself. Make yourself stand out from other teens by seeking more knowledge.

How To Build Your Intellectual Curiosity

The following steps are ways to build your intellectual curiosity:

Ask questions

It is okay to ask questions! Asking intelligent questions will make you a competent teen. When you are not sure of something, ask someone. When you are new to a place, ask how things work there. If you join a new team, ask for the rules. Don't be mute; ask until you know.

Read books

You can build intellectual curiosity by reading books. Almost every topic in the world has a book devoted to it. So, what is stopping you from learning? All the answers you seek are probably hiding on a bookshelf or in ebooks. So, visit the library often or search online for ebooks.

Travel

There is no better way to learn about different places than traveling. Traveling gives you a first-hand experience of what you want to learn. You get to see things yourself and even feel them, if possible. You can plan family trips with your parents. You could also join the group trip you've been avoiding in school. Go to a new location where you can learn new things.

Exercise for intellectual curiosity

Write answers to the following questions.

Choose what your purpose of curiosity is:

- To gain knowledge
- To ensure safety
- For pleasure
- To gain satisfaction

How happy are you to meet new people, read new books, and learn new things?

_____

_____

_____

_____

_____

_____

_____

Time Management

Have you ever laid on your bed at the end of the day and still felt like you've got so much to do despite having the whole day to complete it? If you have, then you're probably not managing your time well.

At a point in high school, I wasn't doing my homework until midnight. I had baseball practice that would not end till late in the evening. By the time I got home, I would be so tired and couldn't do my homework, so I just ate dinner and went to sleep. I was so busy prioritizing other things that I would rush to do my homework at midnight and wake up feeling stressed in the morning. I became distracted in school, and my grades began to suffer.

My teacher got concerned and called my dad's attention to it. My dad knew I wasn't managing my time well and had to speak with my trainer. As a result, I could only attend practice three times a week. Initially, I was angry. But I later understood that my dad had helped me better manage my time and focus on the more important things first.

High school can be very demanding. Numerous activities can take up your time. As a result, learning how to use your time well is essential. Most times, teens get caught up in many unnecessary activities and miss out on the things that matter.

How to Manage Your Time

The following are ways to manage your time effectively:

Prioritize

There would always be an activity to take up your time. It is left to you to determine which ones are the most important. Write down all your activities for the day according to how important they are. Start by doing the most important tasks until you can cover all you need to do. Even if you can't do everything that day, you'll be glad you were able to complete the most important goals.

Cut down on some activities

This should be the quickest way to manage your time. However, cutting down means you will have to let go of those things that take up too much of your time, even if you enjoy doing them.

Engage in activities that lead you to the goals that you have set. For example, if you have no plans to become a singer, you should not be spending three hours a day at singing practice. It will take time away and won't help you in the long run. Instead, focus on activities that help your goals.

Assign time to every task

You should learn to assign time to every activity you have; that will help you stick to your plans. That way, you don't spend more time than necessary on a particular task.

If you plan to spend two hours in the library, make sure you put it down in your journal and don't use more than the specified time. If you want to play video games for an hour, write it down and don't use more than an hour. This will help you know what to do at a particular time.

Exercise for time management

Write answers to the following questions.

What are the unimportant things you waste time on?

_____

_____

_____

_____

_____

_____

_____

_____

How do you feel when you waste your time?

_____

_____

_____

_____

_____

_____

_____

What do you need to do to use your time well?

_____

_____

_____

_____

_____

_____

Write out all that you plan to do today. Arrange each task from the most important to the least important. Focus on doing the important tasks first.

_____

_____

_____

_____

_____

_____

Finding Purpose

During these delicate years of a teenager, many lose sight of their purpose. They try to change their most important aspects to fit into trends. They end up getting confused and falling into depression.

Some of your friends may try to change their purpose because they want to be famous and be referred to as "the cool kid."

Trust me, you are unique and extraordinary. You don't need to follow trends to shine. Your purpose is what you are born to do. No matter what you do, you cannot change your purpose. You need to find your purpose and keep a clear head.

You are different from your friends and others; nobody is made exactly like you. No one can do things the way you do them. You might enjoy engaging in some activities that other teens do not enjoy doing. This does not make you weird in any way. Everyone has their purpose; this is why you should not try to replicate what others are doing. Do you! Don't force yourself to do things just to impress other people.

How to Find Your Purpose

Follow these steps to help find your purpose:

Write out all the things you love to do
Take some time to think deeply about what you really love doing. It might take a day or two but — do it.

What are those things that make you happy when you do them? Write them down. List out all the things you are good at doing. You could also take a clue from what your friends and parents praise you for doing well. They all matter, so write them down.

Arrange them in order of priority

Even though you love doing everything you've written, you may not love each thing equally. Therefore, it is okay to prefer some things over others.

When I was much younger, I loved to dance and would jump on any opportunity to enjoy this part of me. Later, I found out that writing was more therapeutic, and I enjoyed that more. I gradually started to love writing more than I loved dancing, but this didn't stop me from dancing whenever I wanted to. It just meant that I was more interested in writing than dancing.

So, when I jotted down my favorite things to do, writing was at the top of the list. Do this too. Write out what you are good at — from your most favorite to your least favorite.

Pick your purpose

Your purpose lies among the first three things on your list. Look at these carefully and decide which one you want to stick to. It is okay to have more than one purpose in life. No rule says you were born to do only one thing. Choosing your purpose would make life better and easier for you and others around you. You will feel fulfilled when you discover and work toward your purpose.

Exercise for finding purpose

Whatever you choose can be life-changing, so take your time. Think deeply before you write anything down. You could even go for a walk first for peace and clarity.

Write answers to the following questions.

Write down all the activities that make you happy

_____

_____

_____

_____

_____

_____

_____

_____

Now, write them according to how important they are to you. Put the most important ones first.

_____

_____

_____

_____

_____

_____

_____

Write out the first three things on your list and make them your vision and mission.

_____

_____

_____

_____

_____

_____

_____

Employability Skills (How to find a job)

The teenage years come with lots of freedom. You can now go where you want and visit places you were not permitted to go in the past. But freedom isn't isolated; it has a twin responsibility.

Before now, your parents were solely responsible for all your needs. Now that you are a teenager, you need to be more responsible and start planning how to get a job. You may not necessarily need the job now but knowing how to be employable is essential.

If you want to do anything extra – going on short trips, visiting restaurants, and splurging money on expensive clothes – you need a job to fund that.

How to Find a Job

The following are steps on how to find a job:

Decide what kinds of jobs you're interested in

Do not make the mistake of jumping into a job you dislike because you want to make some cash. You might only end up frustrating yourself and messing things up for your employer. For example, if the sight of dirty plates and leftover food irritates you, a job in an eatery is not for you. Instead, make sure that, to some extent, you love the job you are applying for.

It doesn't have to be your favorite job, but a little interest would be okay. For example, if you love washing your dad's car, then maybe you should think of getting a job at the car wash close to your home.

Get yourself ready

You have to get ready to be interviewed at any time. You don't want to meet a potential employer unprepared.

One way to prepare is to arrange your relevant documents in a file. For example, you would need your school ID card, birth certificate, passport, and application letter. You might also need other documents depending on the job specification. If you have any certificate from volunteering in any group, you should add that too. It shows that you have had working experience.

Speak to family and friends

Now that you have what you'll need, it's time to speak to people. Since you have no experience, you will need your parents, neighbors, friends, or your friend's parents to help with any employment opportunity they may have.

Tell everyone you possibly can about the kind of job you want and what makes you fit for it. You may or may not need their influence to land your first job. However, telling people should help give you a great start.

Search online

The world is becoming digital. The internet is there for you to find anything you want. So, if you need a job, you can search online for openings. You should see several openings and options to choose from.

When searching for jobs online, you must check carefully to avoid scamming. Unfortunately, there are many scams on the internet, so keep your guard up.

Sharpen your skills

Before an employer would be willing to give you a job, you have to prove that you are fit for that job. But you may think since it's your first time, and you probably have no experience, how do you show an employer that you're fit for a job? Well, this is where sharpening your skills comes in.

Specific skills are required in any job you want to apply for. For example, you will need skills like eloquence, punctuality, and neatness regardless of where you work. Also, you need to develop active listening, teamwork, effective communication, creative thinking, adaptability, and problem-solving skills. Thankfully, this book explains how to develop these skills.

Exercise for employability skills

Write answers to the following questions.

Where would you love to work?

_____

_____

_____

_____

_____

_____

_____

How do you feel when you have to work on a team?

_____

_____

_____

_____

_____

_____

Search for jobs online and pick the three most appealing to you. Next, carry out research to fill the table below.

The job role	What I would enjoy about this role is...	The skill used in this role that I already have is...	The skill used in the role that I don't have is...
		I will demonstrate that I have this skill by...	I will develop this skill by...
		I will demonstrate that I have this skill by...	I will develop this skill by...
		I will demonstrate that I have this skill by...	I will develop this skill by...

Organizational Skills

Organizational skills are all you need! They make your work faster and easier. Organizational skills are skills that help you learn faster and handle tasks better. These skills will be beneficial when you get a job.

You need organizational skills not only at work but at home too. For example, I notice that whenever my room is cluttered, it makes me feel overwhelmed and tired. So, I make it a habit to constantly keep my space organized. Those little things count.

Some examples of organizational skills are:

- Prioritizing
- Orderliness
- Time Management
- Self-motivation

How To Develop Organizational Skills

To develop organizational skills:

Get a Journal

Journaling will help you keep your day in order. You are more likely to get things done when you write them down. Besides, a journal helps you remember all that must be done so you do not miss anything. So, get a journal, write out what you want to do for the day, and check it from time to time to ensure you're on track.

Use your time wisely

Your inability to use your time well is a big sign of your lack of organizational skills. You cannot have pending assignments to do and sit down to play video games or press your phone all day. It's a waste of time.

Give enough time to the tasks that matter; the less important ones can wait. Once you can plan your time, you are one step closer to being an organized person.

Communicate effectively

Communication is not just about talking nonstop; you have to listen too. Both skills work hand in hand. Being able to communicate wherever you find yourself is an excellent organizational skill.

When you are on a team, patiently communicate your thoughts and suggestions with the other team members. It helps everyone to stay organized too.

Get comfortable with delegating tasks

I used to feel like I could get everything done myself. I wanted to wash my parent's car, do the house chores, lead my class group, be the president of my school press club, and still find time to study. But guess what? It didn't work out at all.

I was always everywhere, doing everything and achieving less. I didn't have time to rest and study well. I was really disorganized. I had to get comfortable assigning tasks to others and letting some things be; I didn't need to be everywhere. It made the work easier and made me more organized.

Exercise for organizational skills

Write answers to the following questions.

	Goal	People that can help me keep track of the goal	What's the backup plan for this goal?	Ways to celebrate reaching this goal
What should I do on Monday?				
What should I do on Tuesday?				
What should I do on Wednesday?				

What should I do on Thursday?				
What should I do on Friday?				
What should I do on Saturday?				
What should I do on Sunday?				

What does an organized person look like? What do they do?

_____

_____

_____

_____

_____

_____

_____

What does a disorganized person look like? What do they do?

_____

_____

_____

_____

_____

_____

_____

What problems do you face when you're disorganized?

_____

_____

_____

_____

_____

_____

_____

Why do you want to be more organized?

_____

_____

_____

_____

_____

_____

_____

What would you start doing to improve your organizational skills?

_____

_____

_____

_____

_____

_____

_____

Driving and Auto Maintenance Skills

I learned how to drive when I was a teenager. All through the ride, I was literally screaming on the wheels. All that mattered at that moment was that I could move the car around. I was so excited.

If you're thinking of learning how to drive soon, you should know that it is not enough to learn how to drive. You should also have general driving knowledge and some auto maintenance skills. These skills help you through the little problems that may arise when you're driving.

Some general driving tips are:

- Don't drink and drive
- Be extra careful when driving in a bad weather
- Always put on your seat belt

- Obey traffic rules
- Adhere to speed limits

Even after sticking to the tips above, your car might still develop issues when you least expect it. You never can tell! However, there are a few tips you can adhere to, and this should ensure your safety.

Always have a spare tire

Getting a flat tire when you least expect it can be annoying. Thankfully, it won't be such a big deal if you have a spare tire handy. Keeping a spare tire in the trunk of your car would save you the embarrassment of being stuck on the road and without help. Always have a good spare tire in your car, especially when driving long distances.

If you find yourself stuck with a flat tire, here's how to change it:

- Pull over to a safe place.
- Check if you have a jack, wrench, and spare tire. These should always be in your car. Additional items that can make the process easier are gloves, flashlight, mat for kneeling, tire gauge, and vehicle manual.
- Start by loosening the lug nuts.
- Lift the vehicle off the ground with a jack.
- Start removing the lug nuts counterclockwise until they are very loose, then remove the tire.
- Use the lug nut posts to align the holes in the spare and place the spare on the wheelbase. Push onto the wheelbase.
- Replace the lug nuts.
- Use the jack to slowly lower your vehicle and finish tightening the lug nuts.
- And you're done!

Change your car oil frequently

One thing you must constantly check in a car is the oil. Check all the fluids before driving out. Clean oil makes your car move swiftly and increases your engine's lifespan. It gives your car a smooth run.

Check the spark plug regularly

If your car has a problem with starting, it may be the spark plugs. Do not wait till the engine light is on and the start sound is unusual before checking the spark plug.

Replace your mirrors

Your side mirrors and rearview mirror are not just to beautify a car — they are essential parts of your car. You should learn to change them immediately if there is a crack. Keeping your mirrors intact will help you drive safely and avoid crashing into vehicles.

Exercise for driving and auto maintenance skills

Write answers to the following questions.

Explain how you felt when you first started driving. If you haven't started driving yet, do you join in on cleaning tasks and simple car repairs at home?

_____

_____

_____

_____

_____

_____

Have you ever had any troubles while driving on the road? How did you handle it?

_____

_____

_____

_____

_____

_____

_____

Going forward, what steps would you take to avoid car troubles?

_____

_____

_____

_____

_____

_____

_____

Emergency and Skills for Staying Safe

Going out with friends is fun, especially now that you have the freedom to do so. However, staying safe is essential when out alone, with friends, in school, or at home.

Everyone needs skills to stay safe, but you need it more as a teen because you are still young, and people can easily prey on young, unsuspecting teens. Hence, you must be on the lookout and ensure you stay safe. Even though your parents can't go everywhere with you, you can ensure your safety by learning basic safety skills.

Tips To Stay Safe

The following tips will help you stay safe:

Let someone know where you are
At every point in time, ensure that your parents know your whereabouts. Always be specific. Include who you are going to see or what you are going to do. If you must leave the location for another place, update your parents.

Do not stay out late
Avoid staying out late. If your parents have given you a curfew, don't stay out past your curfew time. If you have to stay out late, call to inform your parents about where you are and when they should expect you at home.

Avoid talking to strangers
You should be careful about the people you speak to when you are out. Don't assume that only men can harm you. Don't trust strangers, even if they look harmless. Don't reveal any personal information about yourself or your family to anyone.

Do not walk alone in strange places

If you are going to a new place, always go with someone. If you can't get an older person to go with you, go in groups of three or four. Don't use earbuds outside your home. Make sure you can always hear what is being said around you.

Use social media responsibly

Be very careful about the information you put out about yourself on social media. Anyone can access your private information by simply clicking on your profile. Also, never agree to meet up physically with someone you met online. If you need to do so, inform your parents about it first.

What to do in an emergency

Emergencies are usually chaotic since they happen unexpectedly. Losing your composure and being confused about the appropriate action is not uncommon during an emergency. Therefore, it is essential that you have a basic idea of what to do during an emergency. Have a list of what to do, whether at school or anywhere else. This way, you are confident, knowing how to handle yourself and those around you. Emergency situations are different. However, the following are basic guidelines that should help you.

During an emergency, you should:

- Remain calm to allow yourself to think clearly and not act based on emotions.

- Evaluate the situation for danger.

- Access the scenario for danger; then you can decide whether it is safe to leave the place or shelter in place.

- If you've safely evacuated or sheltered in place, you can

call for help using 911. Explain everything you know about the situation.

- If there's any injured person, provide first aid, then move them away from danger.

- Obtain any information you can without endangering yourself. Then brief the emergency responders on every detail when they arrive at the scene.

- Do not hide in a dark place. Make sure you stay in public places and in sight of other people.

- If you notice that someone is chasing you, scream for help. Do not stop screaming until you can get people's attention for yourself.

Remember, when there is an emergency, the priority should be safety. You can minimize potential danger and stabilize the incident when you ensure your safety.

Exercise for dealing with emergencies

Write answers to the following questions.

How do you know that an environment is unsafe for you?

_____

_____

_____

_____

_____

_____

What do you do to stay away from places that feel unsafe?

_____

_____

_____

_____

_____

_____

Basic Educational Skills

Knowing how to read, write, and do basic calculations is an essential skill every teen should have. Moreover, it gives you the upper hand when searching for certain opportunities.

If you want to relate well with people, you have to have some simple educational skills such as how to read, write, do basic math, and know how to use the computer. With educational skills, you can engage in conversations with others.

How to Develop Basic Educational Skills

The following are ways to develop basic educational skills.

Take your books seriously
Read your books daily. You'll definitely pick up important information that will be helpful to you in school and the outside world; reading keeps you informed.

Know basic math

You do not need to memorize how the elevation and depression of an angle are calculated to feel you've gained educational skills. However, you need to know how to do basic addition, subtraction, multiplication, and division.

Exercise for basic educational skills

What activities do you engage in that make you book smart?

_____

_____

_____

_____

_____

_____

How do you plan to improve your reading, writing, and basic calculation skills?

_____

_____

_____

_____

_____

Domestic Skills - Managing a Home

Can you make your meals yourself? Do you leave your room dirty? How often do you clean your water tank?

All your life, you've probably had someone doing chores for you. It is time to learn how to do some basic domestic tasks and take charge when needed.

How to Manage a Home

Managing a home shouldn't be difficult after reading the tips below:

Keep your space tidy
Nobody wants to study or rest in an unkempt room. A dirty room will leave you unmotivated. You won't feel inclined to study and do your homework effectively.

Keeping your workspace neat and attractive will increase your productivity. You will feel very comfortable, and your body and mind will feel relaxed.

Organize your belongings
Do not give in to that voice telling you to take your clothes and shoes and drop them carelessly. Instead, hang or fold your clothes well, keep your shoes on the racks, and put utensils where they should be. Put every item where it belongs and see how organized your room will look.

Learn how to prepare common dishes
I have always loved cooking. I used to help my mum whenever she made meals for the family. So, it is no surprise that I am very creative with the meals I cook now. Of course, eating out

occasionally isn't a bad idea, but cooking at home saves us a lot of money.

Learning to cook allows you to prepare the kind of food you'd like to eat at any time. Besides, home-cooked meals are healthier.

Exercise for managing a home

What do you think makes your room look untidy?

_____

_____

_____

_____

_____

_____

What can you do to make sure that your room stays clean?

_____

_____

_____

_____

_____

_____

Don't you find it interesting that all these universal skills are interconnected? You will find one skill being very useful in another. That's the way it works. You will find your teenage years more interesting if you take note of the skills in this chapter.

CHAPTER 3
BUSINESS SKILLS

Business skills are essential to starting, operating, and managing a successful business. If you desire to own a business, these skills will help you satisfy your customer's needs when it's time. Even as an employee, business skills let you stand out from the competition and enhance your career.

Everyone has been involved in business, whether directly or indirectly. I remember convincing my dad to let me clean his shoes in exchange for a dollar bill. That was business, at least for someone of my age back then.

If you plan to start a business, you might as well do it properly. Doing business without the right attitude would keep you at the losing end. But, thanks to business skills, teenagers can put ideas into action. It stimulates the area of your brain responsible for risk-taking and creativity. It also teaches you how to direct and manage teams to complete tasks.

What Are Business Skills?

Business skills are skills needed when running a business or at work. It is how you can relate with your friends or teammates when you have to work with them. These soft skills will help you understand your teammates and others you need to interact with.

These skills are needed for the success of any team. This is why employers are always looking for people with business skills. So, before you apply for any job, ensure that you have the business skills needed to work in the organization.

These skills cannot be learned in a day. Instead, you have to slowly build them through consistent practice.

To succeed in the business world, you will need skills like:

Decision-Making Skills

Teenagers make decisions every single day! It starts when you are given a modest choice between two options, such as when your mum asks if you want tea or coffee.

Decision-making is not as complex as it sounds. It is just a simple act of choosing what step to take after carefully considering all the factors involved. It means carefully studying all your options and making the right choice afterward.

Although decision-making is easy, you might still find it very tough to decide what to do when you are left alone. Sometimes, this is because right from childhood your parents have always decided what you should do, leaving you with no other choice. So, choosing what you want is still very new to you.

Other times, it is because you have not learned the necessary steps to take before coming to a conclusion. So, you try not to make decisions so that you do not take the blame for any mistakes.

Recent studies suggest that teens who can assess a situation and come to a reasonable conclusion are more successful. This is why you must build up this skill from a young age.

Some teenagers make decisions based on what seems to be trending. They do not understand what their choices would mean to them in the end. They just go with the flow because it feels right at the moment; this is how they get into a lot of trouble.

When I got into college, the whole place seemed new to me. On my first night in the dormitory, one of my roommates offered me a cigarette. I was left confused because I had never been in that situation before. I was left to decide for myself, and I chose to stay away from drugs. This decision has helped me maintain good health even today. This is how important making the right decision is for every teen.

When you have the right decision-making skills, it will protect you from making mistakes that you would end up regretting. Making the right decisions puts you on the right path to achieving your goals.

When you enter the business space, proper decision-making skills will make you employable. It makes you think about what your choices could mean for you and your team.

How to Make Decisions

The following are steps for how to make good decisions:

Define the problem

Knowing your "why" is the first step to decision-making. You need to understand why you need to make that decision. Ask yourself what the problem you want to solve is and why making a decision matters. If you do not decide, what would go wrong? Why does this issue bother you? What is it about the situation that makes it hard for you to decide? Is the problem due to your own actions?

Once you can answer these questions, your problem is defined. Be clear about the problem you want to solve. This gives you a sense of clarity and makes the whole process much easier.

Know your options

The fact that you have to decide means you have a list of options to choose from. If there were only one option, making a decision wouldn't matter because you wouldn't have a choice anyway.

If you think that your options would not solve the problem, then brainstorm and come up with other possible choices. Try to be as creative as you can. You can ask your parents for guidance and suggestions.

Evaluate your options

Before you make a choice, find out how this decision may

affect you and those involved in the long run. Then, if you feel stuck or unsure, you could seek guidance from your parents.

Think about the pros and cons when you decide to go ahead with your choice, and be sure you can handle the consequences your choice may bring.

Choose one option

After careful thinking and deliberation, you need to come to a final conclusion. Choose an option that has many benefits and aligns with your goals.

Would your choice help you achieve your goal? Would it harm someone else? Is it realistic? Be sure that it is the right choice for you.

Go ahead with your plan

This is the part that many teens ignore. If you make a decision, you must be bold enough to make sure that you follow it through. There is no point in going around options and not sticking to one.

When you choose an option, you must take steps to ensure that your decision is followed.

Exercise for decision-making skills

What are some hindrances that make decision-making challenging for you?

_____

_____

_____

_____

_____

_____

When you make decisions and stick by them, how do you feel?

_____

_____

_____

_____

_____

_____

What did you learn about yourself after making an important decision?

_____

_____

_____

_____

_____

_____

Do you ever regret having made a decision in the past? Does that affect how you make decisions now?

_____

_____

_____

_____

_____

_____

_____

Analytical Skills

As humans, everything we do is a result of some decisions that we have made. As days pass by, you will always have to make more decisions. For example, what you eat, when you sleep, what you drink, and every other thing you do. These decisions might be very easy because you have absolute control over them, and they affect only you.

You wake up, brush your teeth, take a shower, pick out nice clothes, and go to school. This decision-making chain is very easy and smooth. However, it gets more challenging when you have to make decisions that would not only affect you but others too. These decisions are harder to make and require a lot of thinking processes that will help you avoid terrible mistakes that hurt you and others. This is exactly where analytical skills are helpful.

What Are Analytical Skills?

Analytical skills are those qualities that help you to observe and interpret situations and ideas so that you can respond with helpful solutions. It helps you think deeply about how your decisions can affect the present and future of others.

Some teenagers make better decisions. They seem to always be accurate in whatever choices they make. What makes them stand out is their analytical skills. Having analytical skills forces you to think critically. It makes you analyze situations based on facts, not feelings or desires.

Analytical skills can be used in your day-to-day activities. They are useful both at home and school.

Some examples of analytical skills are:

- Critical thinking
- Problem-solving
- Resource management
- Collaboration

How Can Analytical Skills Help You?

Have you ever wondered why great scholars like Karl Marx, Aristotle, Socrates, and many others are philosophers? It is because they are critical thinkers (philosophers).

When you have analytical skills, you can consider more facts, risks, and probabilities before you make decisions. All these will guide you and help you to not make decisions based on emotions.

When you start working, you will be in charge of certain responsibilities. Analytical skills would help you perform these duties properly. They will also guide you to make positive decisions for short and long-term benefits.

Teens with analytical skills have been found to make well-thought-out decisions. They do not make choices on impulse. Instead, they think well and analyze before coming to a conclusion.

Having analytical skills will make you think deeply before saying or doing anything. Once you have these skills, all you need to do is apply them to your everyday activities, and life will become easier.

Most teens will automatically get frustrated and stressed out when problems are around them; it is natural to feel this way, but it becomes unwise when you dwell on the problems without seeking solutions.

Instead of joining the group of teens who choose to complain, your analytical skills will help you solve problems without stress. It helps you to save time and money.

Though it sounds technical, analytical skills are very easy to learn. You need to ask the right questions, deliberate on the answers you get, take action, and get the problem solved.

Analytical skills will help you identify the best solutions to problems that come your way. They also make it easy to use your time productively.

One skill that is used hand in hand with analytical skills is good communication. It is essential to be in constant communication with people around. It might be your roommate, neighbor, family member, friends, or colleagues at work.

Communication is very important for identifying a problem and searching for a solution. There is no way you can try to identify, analyze, or solve problems if your communication skills are not in order.

Things to Consider When Analyzing Situations

To effectively analyze a situation, you must assess inner and outer factors. They are very important when you are analyzing because these factors determine how well you understand a situation. They are:

Strengths and Weaknesses: Your strengths are your strong points and assets. The weaknesses are those points that are not too strong and can improve.

Opportunities and Threats: Opportunities are ways that can help you improve and get better. Threats are those elements that could hurt you. They should be avoided or eliminated.

Steps in Analyzing Situations

I once decided to start a business and began studying my environment to find out what service people around me needed.

I made sure that I was interested in the research so that the whole process would be easier for me to go through.

When my research was done, I noticed there were very few photographers in my area. This was in line with my interest, and I decided to seek more knowledge and improve so I might develop my own photography brand.

You might decide to start your own business, run a logistics company, or even get a corporate job. You cannot do any of these things well without having analytical skills. You will need these skills to run the business properly when you start it.

Let's dive into the steps you should take when analyzing situations.

Identify the problem
The first step is problem identification.

There is no need to search for solutions to problems that do not exist. Instead, you need to identify the problem before taking any other step. Then, you need to observe what people need. Once the problem is identified, you can now use the skills you have to find solutions to the identified problems.

Understand the problem
Do not forget that you cannot solve something you do not understand.

I needed to thoroughly analyze to understand that the people in my environment were in need of skilled photographers.

You should do this in your own field too. Take your time to understand the problems so that you do not waste your time and effort on projects that do not matter.

Gather as much information as you can. If you need help, it would do well to ask. Do not believe you can do it all alone.

Consider the people involved
The next step to take is to do an analysis of those people involved in the problem. It could be your customers, colleagues, or whoever.

How would whatever decision you make affect the people around you? Would it be harmful to you too? Would it solve a problem or make things worse?

You need to identify the kind of people you are dealing with, what they want, their preferences, how they behave, their interests, and their challenges. This would keep your information properly organized, and analyzing the situation would be much easier.

Get your resources

No matter how small a problem is, you need the necessary resources to solve it. It could be cash, information, suggestions, references, and lots more.

One crucial question for you is, "Will the resources I have be enough to tackle this problem?" If your answer is "yes," then carry on. But if your answer is negative, then you need to work on getting the necessary resources to help you out.

This would prevent you from starting a task and leaving it unfinished because you are stuck and short of the necessary resources.

Meet people and seek their assistance. For example, you can gather information from your parents or others who have been in your position before.

Weigh your risks

Consider the possible outcomes of your actions; place them on a mental scale and pick the one that best suits your course.

Weed out the options that would leave your team with loss or regrets. For example, if you decide to start a project, how sure are you that it would bring profits to your team? Conversely, can you afford the losses that might occur if your project flops?

Think of all the possible risks and decide if this is something you are willing to embark on. Do not analyze any situation using sentiment as a yardstick — that is risky. Instead, use established facts to weigh your risks.

Establish feasible goals

When analyzing, it is important to consider only achievable goals. Prioritize fixing those issues that pose a big threat to your success and ensure they are adequately tackled. Don't waste time on goals that will not help grow you or your business.

Cut out projects or areas that are not profitable to you or your clients. These things will only ruin your business instead of adding value.

Take action

Now that you have weighed your risks, it is time to take action. When doing this, you will have to come up with plans and strategies to tackle the problem.

As someone running a business or leading a team, you should know that your team is not only about you. It also involves every customer and client you have.

You must consider your opponents, teammates, work environment, and, most importantly, your customers. You have to bring your analytical skills into reality. Now is the time to make moves!

Block loopholes, answer important questions, consider those around you in the same business line, and put yourself in a better position to compete. After analyzing a situation, your actions should be able to answer the questions below.

Economical: What are the financial effects of your actions? Will the decision yield profits or losses for the business?

Sociological: Are the cultural movement and trends for or against you? These are important considerations to make when analyzing situations.

In the course of your actions, you have to remain positive, focused, and motivated. These will keep you going.

If you find yourself in a team, keep it engaged and carry it along. Keep your team motivated and keep their eyes on the end result. Make sure you listen to ideas that your teammates might suggest.

Analytical skills are not just for decision-making. Use it to get yourself or your team creative. Ditch boring and mundane ideas!

Once something does not seem to be working, talk it out and make amends. The end objective is to achieve what goal has been set.

You will encounter challenges in whatever you do. In fact, challenges are a big part of every business. These could be challenges like strengths, weaknesses, opportunities, and threats, and you wouldn't know where to start.

Do not allow the challenges to hinder you from moving. Overthinking will only make you feel worse and dampen your vibe. Instead, take things step by step.

Learn to prioritize. This will help you to focus more on pressing issues.

If you use your analytical skills well, your business will improve, and your team will get better too.

Remember the group of people I mentioned earlier in this chapter who choose to lament and get frustrated when they encounter problems? Do not be a member of that group.

When these challenges spring up, think about them critically, analyze them, solve them, and use them as steppingstones until you get the desired result.

Exercise for analyzing situations

How do you feel when you judge a situation based on how you feel at the moment?

_____

_____

_____

_____

_____

_____

Write out all the things you consider before you make a decision.

_____

_____

_____

_____

_____

_____

_____

How has thinking analytically affected your relationships with people?

_____

_____

_____

_____

_____

_____

_____

Adaptability

Some years back, I had a mini-reunion with some of my high school friends who had traveled worldwide. We had a fun time and ended the day with a conversation. They all shared their experiences and how they struggled to settle into new environments with cultures and lifestyles they weren't used to. They had to adapt to the environment after some time.

This showed me how important adaptability skills are and why they are essential to our personal and business lives.

What is Adaptability?

Adaptability is when you can adjust to new conditions with a positive mindset. It is when you can take a new shape to fit into the new circumstances and come up with a solution. For businesses, adaptability could mean the ability to quickly change to stay ahead of the competition.

Teenage life is very uncertain, and there is no better way to navigate than having adaptability skills. It helps you blend in quickly and thrive despite the changes around you. You will grow to become an adult that can work either physically or remotely.

Businesses need to be ready to adapt if they want to survive. Any business that can't keep up with change will fail in a constantly evolving world. In your workplace, things will not always go as expected. This is why most employers prefer to hire someone they can trust to sort things out when they go south.

You cannot prevent change from happening, but you have power over how you respond to it. Every worker works and thinks uniquely. Your ability to adapt will help you accept and recognize that. It will also help you connect with people whose personalities are different from yours.

Some essential adaptability skills that you should have in a business space are:

- Communication
- Problem-solving
- Resourcefulness
- Stress management
- Decision-making
- Organization

How is Adaptability Helpful to You?

Imagine that a co-worker calls in sick, and you have to cover up for them. A teen with adaptability skills will see the new task as a challenge rather than something to make a fuss about.

When you are adaptable, unexpected changes don't leave you

anxious. You simply try to make the most out of the situation. This does not mean you should lose yourself and your purpose or continually take on other people's duties. It simply suggests that you can find a balance and make everyday changes work in your favor. Being adaptable exposes you to lots of opportunities. It puts you a step ahead of others.

How Can You Become Adaptable?

The following are ways you can become adaptable:

Learn quickly

Things will eventually change, and they won't remain stagnant no matter how good you are at what you do. Your job description will change, the colleagues you are used to working with will change, and even the tools you work with will change. However, you must learn to move quickly to remain relevant despite the changes.

No employer wants to keep repeating procedures and instructions over and over. So do your research, make inquiries, and be eager to know more. Being inquisitive and learning quickly is a great step toward becoming adaptable.

Help to solve problems

Every employer wants an adaptable person because they can solve problems effortlessly. There is no point in being in an organization if you aren't helping to solve a problem. You were employed to solve a particular problem, so do it well.

If an unexpected issue arises at work, ensure you can pop up a suggestion to solve the problem or at least help to ease the situation. While helping to solve the problem, do it with a cheerful face, not a grumpy one.

Be receptive to change

You should not be rigid if you plan to run a successful business. Rigidity will cause a lot of opportunities to pass you by. Just move with time. Be open to change; not just any kind of change, but a positive one. This will go a long way to help you become adaptable. Don't be scared to try out new things or take risks. You'll never know what you are capable of if you don't try. Try out new things and see whether they will work out or not.

Change course

When one path does not seem to work, will you choose to remain there, hoping for a miracle? No. This will only make you stagnant. Always be ready to change course. Once you notice a plan is not working, switch to another that works. Be ready to change when things don't go as planned. Do not waste time on plans that don't work.

Exercise for adaptability

How does change make you feel?

_____

_____

_____

_____

_____

_____

_____

What new steps would you take to make yourself adaptable?

_____

_____

_____

_____

_____

_____

_____

Some good ways I can deal with change is by...

_____

_____

_____

_____

_____

_____

_____

I will not deal with change by...

_____

_____

_____

_____

_____

_____

_____

Thinking on Your Feet

You are in the middle of a conversation, and suddenly, you draw a blank. The words you were going to say won't come to mind, and you lose your train of thought. You don't know what to say next, so you feel self-conscious and a little embarrassed. Can you relate to this scenario?

This could be a frustrating experience, but it can be worked on and fixed with constant practice.

When you hear somebody say, *"Think on your feet,"* it simply means to react quickly. It means that you can do things well without prior preparation.

Thinking on your feet will help you stay calm and confident, especially when under pressure. You will feel confident enough to respond when random questions are thrown at you.

Are you that student that never goes wrong when asked questions in class? Do you read ahead of your teacher and always deliver the right answers even when unprepared? If yes, then you are someone who thinks on their feet; every time, you do or say something correctly even when you aren't prepared for it. This is exactly what thinking on your feet is.

Thinking on your feet means making the right decisions even when you are scared and unprepared. Confidence is essential for you to think on your feet.

Imagine that your teacher asks you a question in class. You know the answer but are not confident enough to stand up and say it. You haven't shown that you can think on your feet, even though you can.

You cannot properly show that you can think on your feet without being confident. These two skills go hand in hand. To think on your feet is to be confident enough to show that your words, actions, and decisions will solve a problem.

How do I think on my feet?

Thinking on your feet is not as difficult as it seems. It is like any random skill that can be learned. Here are some tips to guide you.

Be Calm

You will feel nervous when you are under pressure. It is normal to feel that way. But for a teen who hopes to become a better person, you should not stay that way for long. You must be calm and allow your brain to process the information or questions before you.

Try your best to stay relaxed. Take deep breaths, count to ten, and process your thoughts well before responding. Never jump impulsively at questions when you are under pressure; it never ends well.

Listen well

After confidence, listening is another skill you should have in your pocket. Why do you need to listen? To ensure that you fully know and understand whatever question or request is placed before you.

If you don't listen well before you reply, you might give wrong answers, and the pressure will mount. Listening will help you to know what you should and should not say in response to whatever has been said or done.

Do not interrupt, even if you think you know the response to the question being asked. It is not courteous to do that. It only implies that whatever you are being told means nothing to you. If you need more time to think, request that the question be repeated. Doing this makes you look really interested in the topic in question.

Always be on your guard

Day-to-day experiences are not scripted. What does this tell you? It means that the things you expect may not go as you think they will. This is why you need to always be prepared. Always read ahead and dig for information on topics related to your line of interest. For example, if you are interested in technology, you should have basic knowledge about innovations. You never can tell when this information will come in handy.

Consider doing some findings on the business skills that people in your field have and the qualities that the hiring managers are looking for. Then, decide which skills you possess and which ones you need to work on.

Be creative

As much as you try to be very careful with your words, you should also be creative enough to keep the conversation going. Avoid using polar responses. These are "yes" and "no" responses. When you give polar responses, it may show that you are not interested in the conversation.

When you are confronted with questions you are unsure of, wait a while and think properly before giving a proper response. If you must respond with yes or no, add extra information. This makes you sound sure of what you are saying. For example, if your mom asks if you are done with the task she gave you, rather than simply saying *"no,"* you could say, *"I am almost done with the task. When I complete it, I will definitely let you know."*

Be a tactician

Being a tactician doesn't mean you should use the 4-4-2 tactics on the football pitch. Here, the tactic you need to apply is the delay tactic. The delay tactic is repeating the question to yourself in the best way you understand.

Repeat the question to yourself and understand it before you give a reply. The worst mistake you can make when asked a question is to say whatever comes to your mind first without understanding the question. Most times, you will end up sounding disorganized and unintelligent. Don't do it.

You can rephrase the question and elicit a positive response when you use the delay tactic. If needed, ask for clarification or even a definition.

Use your moment of silence wisely

Those few seconds of silence before you respond to any question can end in either a good or a bad way, depending on how you choose to use them. Do not use that moment of silence to panic or allow bad thoughts to overwhelm you. The answers are within, but you will say the wrong things if you rush to answer. By the time you realize it, it may be too late.

Do not pretend

People do not always like to admit that they don't have correct answers to questions. They do this to protect their ego and look smart. It is okay if you do not have the answer to a question immediately. No one knows it all, after all.

If you do not have a correct reply to a question you are asked, just be plain about it. You can say, *"I'm not sure I have a solution to this situation. If you could give me some time, I would come up with something that might help."*

You may look foolish when you try to play smart and claim you know what you are saying even when you know you are wrong.

Keep an open mind

You must be open-minded if you want to learn to think on your feet. Do not keep a rigid mindset when interacting with people. You have to learn to take new suggestions from people; this will open your mind to new possibilities. That does not mean that you should totally discard your own thoughts — it just means that you should be willing to take suggestions.

Practice regularly

Do not believe that you can always have your way out without putting in any effort. Nothing good comes easily. Instead, you have to try first. Use your mental imaginations to practice. If you have close friends, get them to ask you random questions. Use moments like that to practice and get better. As time goes on, you will become a pro at thinking on your feet.

Planning for everything life throws at you is a waste of time as it is practically impossible. You can't be totally prepared for everything, but you can get ready to deal with whatever comes.

Work on building your confidence; be focused and devote time to preparing for likely situations. Being confident does not mean you are immune to fear or getting scared. Neither does it exempt you from making mistakes. Instead, confidence means you are willing to trust your abilities and still try, even when you feel anxious or scared. So, take that step and begin to work on your confidence. This will make a big difference.

When working with a team and the members see how calmly you handle moments of pressure, they will trust you, and you will earn their respect. This will help you soar higher.

Exercise for thinking on your feet

How do you feel when you answer questions impulsively?

_____

_____

_____

_____

_____

_____

_____

What steps would you take to ensure that you are employable?

_____

_____

_____

_____

_____

_____

What are the qualities you have that can boost your confidence?

_____

_____

_____

_____

_____

_____

_____

CHAPTER 4
ENTREPRENEURIAL SKILLS

"Any time is a good time to start a company."
- Ron Conway

Thanks to the internet, anyone can start a business from the comfort of their room. You aren't too young to start a business. In fact, starting a business as a teen comes with many benefits because it allows you to make mistakes and learn from them without suffering severe consequences. It helps build you up for the future.

Teens are getting recognized worldwide and making a name for themselves by engaging in activities they enjoy. They search for things that people are interested in and sell them. They can do these things because they use entrepreneurial skills properly.

Entrepreneurial skills help teenagers start up and manage businesses successfully. They are essential skills that every teen who hopes to have a successful business should have.

Managing a business isn't just about telling people what you do. It takes a lot more. But, with entrepreneurial skills, teenagers can easily decide which line of business suits them, attract the right audience, and keep customers coming back for more.

The following worksheet will help you identify the best business for you.

List some activities that you enjoy doing in your leisure

1. _____

2. _____

3. _____

4. _____

5. _____

6. _____

7. _____

8. _____

Why do you feel happy about these activities?

1. _____

2. _____

3. _____

4. _____

5. _____

6. _____

7. _____

8. _____

List out the types of businesses that are related to these activities

Job role	I like it because	I don't like it because
Dancer	It makes me fit	I sweat a lot after dancing

Now, write out which job(s) you think you can cope with

1. _____

2. _____

3. _____

4. _____

5. _____

Some entrepreneurial skills that will help you manage a business well are:

1. _____

2. _____

3. _____

4. _____

5. _____

Self-Confidence

The world is moving at breakneck speed; changes occur every day, and anyone who is not confident in their skills will be run over. Teenagers need self-confidence the most because they are new to the rapid changes in themselves and their environment. You need to be confident to stand firm with what you believe in and not go just anywhere the wind blows.

Self-confidence is a skill that any teen who wants to succeed in today's world must have. You must be confident in yourself — your body, skills, and ideas. Self-confidence is something that most teenagers struggle with. Some teens wrongly believe that they must force their opinions on others to show confidence. But confidence is not shutting out other people's voices because you think yours is the best.

Self-confidence is believing in yourself. It means that you feel good about your abilities, skills, and boundaries and aren't scared to tell others about them. You can convince another person to believe your idea or suggestion is good only if you are confident. On the other hand, no one will think you are genuine if you are unsure or scared to tell people about your ideas.

How to Build Self-Confidence

It may take weeks, months, or even years, but self-confidence can be learned. You need to work on your mind when you want to build your self-confidence. Train your mind to be consistent and disciplined; this will do you good on this journey.

Avoid toxic people and places
Whether platonic or romantic, relationships bring out the best part of you and do not make you feel incapable. This is why you

should stay with people who believe in you and support your goals.

The people you spend time with will affect how you feel about yourself. So, it is wise to reconsider your relationship with someone who constantly disrespects you or makes you feel bad about yourself.

Feeling confident in your abilities is difficult when people criticize you more than they compliment you. This is because the discouraging words they say to you might stay in your head and affect what you think of yourself.

You should avoid situations, places, people, or things that make you feel bad about your skills and ideas. Reduce your interactions with them or keep them out of your life completely. This does not imply that you should resist criticism and advice from others. Instead, you should learn to distinguish between those who correct you in love and those who just want to spite you.

Stick with friends who appreciate and say nice words to you when you do good and correct you patiently when you do bad.

Take breaks from social media

All the different opinions on social media have the potential to be harmful to your self-confidence. It might be time to take a break from social media if you compare your life to people's perfectly staged photographs.

Regular breaks from the internet would help you stay sane and at peace with yourself. Concentrate your efforts on things that bring you joy. Take a stroll with a friend, read a book, or enjoy quality time with family.

Say positive things to yourself

You're the most important person in your world and what you believe about yourself is what primarily matters. This is why you have to be conscious about the things you think in your mind.

Say positive affirmations to yourself often, and you will start to believe and act them out. Don't be too hard on yourself. Although it might feel strange at first, speaking positive affirmations to yourself will turn out to be really helpful in boosting your self-confidence.

Accept that you are not perfect

No one will ever be perfect. However, the earlier you accept that you have your own flaws, just like everyone else, the stronger your self-confidence will be. Teens who make perfection their main goal could feel dismissive about everything else. This would undermine teammates' efforts and cause frustration when things didn't turn out exactly how the person wanted them to be.

Keep trying to get better, but do not let perfection define you. Instead, enjoy your mistakes and try your best to correct them if you can.

Live a healthy life

Your lifestyle is connected to your mood and how you feel about yourself. For example, healthy food like greens and grains will leave you feeling good. They also help keep your body in good shape. Junk food, on the other hand, will mess with your mood and make you feel tired.

Consciously make an effort to reduce your intake of junk food. Instead, feed your body nutritious foods to feel better and have more energy. Daily exercise boosts your health, releases happy hormones, and makes you feel better. In addition, your body and your confidence will benefit from proper exercise and enough sleep.

Exercise for self-confidence

Ten things I love about myself are:

1. _____

2. _____

3. _____

4. _____

5. _____

6. _____

7. _____

8. _____

9. _____

10. _____

Ten things I am proud to have achieved are:

1. _____

2. _____

3. _____

4.. _____

5. _____

6. _____

7. _____

8. _____

9. _____

10. _____

Five things that crush my confidence and how to avoid them are:

Things that crush my confidence

1. _____

2. _____

3. _____

4. _____

5. _____

I will avoid them by

1. _____

2. _____

3. _____

4. _____

5. _____

A compliment to myself is:

_____

_____

_____

_____

_____

_____

_____

Problem-Solving Skills

Every teen faces problems one way or the other. It doesn't matter whether they are small or big ones — what makes a problem is a "problem." As days pass, you will need to stop depending on your parents at all times and solve your problems yourself. For instance, you will meet different people when you get into high school or college. They will have opinions and behaviors that you don't entirely agree with. But, again, this shouldn't lead to an exchange of words or a physical fight.

Arguments might put tension into your relationship with these people, and it becomes a problem in the long run. Nobody is coming to solve your problems for you. You have to find a way to solve them yourself.

You have two options to choose from when you are faced with difficult situations: you can decide to flee, or you can find a solution. Running away is not the best course of action because the problems still linger even after you run.

Problem-solving skills teach you to face your problems head-on and completely eliminate them. As a result, they are the most sought-after skills in school, social, and work environments.

No teen is born with problem-solving skills, so you need to train yourself to learn them. It can be tricky to work around this because it requires you to challenge yourself. But it's always worth it.

Developing excellent problem-solving skills will help you sort out your personal problems. You will also be able to solve some other people's problems. Ultimately, it will reassure you that you matter and have much to offer your friends, family members, and everyone around you. The world will roll in excitement at your feet. It has no choice!

What Are Problem-Solving Skills?

Problem-solving skills are those qualities that help you to know why a problem keeps occurring and how to resolve that problem.

What's happening? Why is it happening? How do I solve this issue?

These questions are what teens with problem-solving skills typically ask. Problem-solving skills are beneficial; the reason is simple. Teens that have this quality can handle difficult or unexpected circumstances very easily.

Some teenagers solve problems like a pro. You might seem surprised that they know their way around numerous complex situations. The secret to this power is problem-solving skills. Having problem-solving skills spurs you to think critically. It will help you know how to spot problems, understand them, and develop relevant solutions.

Problem-solving skills can be used in your everyday life. However, you need to develop this skill to quickly craft solutions when encountering problems.

Some examples of problem-solving skills are:

- Decision-making
- Creativity
- Critical thinking
- Teamwork
- Research
- Active listening
- Excellent communication
- Flexibility
- Patience

How Are Problem-Solving Skills Helpful to You?

If you want to excel at anything, you need problem-solving skills. Without these, your options are limited, and you'll be lucky to avoid spending the night alone in your room with nothing to offer. This does not mean that teens that haven't developed these skills do not matter. It's just reality staring at you. The world needs more problem-solvers.

When you start your business, you must manage some situations yourself; problem-solving skills will help you to handle them properly. However, not all problem-solving involves responding to the problems you see around you. It can also mean creating new ideas and improving the area around you.

Your ability to solve problems will help you to identify and seize opportunities to make yourself and everyone around you happy. Teenagers with strong problem-solving skills have successfully handled complex problems in familiar and foreign environments. They do not limit themselves. Instead, they listen well, think calmly, and understand tasks before concluding.

Excellent problem-solvers can easily fit into problem-solving careers such as judges, marketing directors, attorneys, physicians, computer programmers, and many others. So, if you pursue these careers with your problem-solving skills, you will find it easier than others that don't have this ability will.

Steps to Solving a Problem Effectively

The following are steps to take to become an effective problem-solver:

What's the Problem?
The first step in solving a problem is figuring out the issue. You need to be sure of your needs and what other people need. This way, you can come up with relevant solutions to the problem. You can identify the problem by asking the people involved for their opinions. Questionnaires and surveys would also make identifying the problem easier for you.

Why Is it an Issue?
It's not enough to identify the issue. You need to think well

and determine why it's a problem. When you find out why it is a problem, it will be easier for you to come to a solution. The following questions can guide you:

- Why do you want this?
- Why is this project so dear to you and your team?
- Why does it bother you?
- What's the worst that could happen if it is not solved?

With these questions answered, you can figure out the root of the problem.

What Are the Possible Solutions to the Issue?

There are different types of solutions to different problems. This means that what may solve one problem may not solve the other. This is why it's important to develop brainstorming skills.

Brainstorming requires you to list as many ideas as possible, no matter how irrelevant they may seem. Of course, you could set the stage by making an extreme suggestion first. Sometimes, extreme measures can end up unleashing more helpful options.

For instance, suppose your parents are not too comfortable with you pursuing an Esports career. Then, you could try out the following possible solutions.

- Practice Esports at home to show your parents how committed you are to learning.
- Watch the games on TV at your house to familiarize your parents with them.
- Read magazines and other helpful materials on Esports and show them to your parents.
- Think of counterarguments to sway your parents' decision.

For example, most parents don't want their kids to be Esports players because they don't see it as a career path.

What Are the Pros and Cons of the Solutions?

At this point, you can turn in your list of solutions to other people, like members of your family or team members, for review. Besides their reviews, you should also make your evaluation.

When you have a list of upsides and downsides, you can remove the solutions that have more disadvantages. Now rank each solution on a scale of 0 to 10. In this way, you can find the most favorable ones.

Sometimes, you might be unable to find a solution that makes everyone happy. But you should be able to find one that everyone can adjust to. Once you've set the plan in motion, you need to check how it's going. Remember that some solutions need time to work.

Give it some time, and if it doesn't work, try some more solutions. One of the most significant parts of problem-solving skills is persistence. You need to be able to go back to the drawing board if things don't go as expected.

Exercise for problem-solving

Some problems I think people around me face are:

1. _____

2. _____

3. _____

What are the causes of these problems?

1. _____

2. _____

3. _____

List three possible solutions to each of these problems and state the pros and cons of each

Problems	Possible three solutions	Pros	Cons	The best solution
1.	•			
	•			
	•			

2.	•			
	•			
	•			
3.	•			
	•			
	•			

What would you do to make this solution work?

1. _____

2. _____

3. _____

4. _____

5. _____

What would you do if your solutions didn't work out?

_____

_____

_____

_____

_____

_____

_____

_____

Initiative

"The best way to not feel hopeless is to get up and do something. Don't wait for good things to happen to you. If you go out and make some good things happen, you will fill the world with hope, you will fill yourself with hope." ~ **Barack Obama**

Difficult times bring out the worst in us and could, in many cases, reduce us to the lowest point of our life. An excellent way to overcome this situation is to remember that, *"It is better to be proactive and not reactive."*

When you were a child, you used to wait for your parents to make important decisions. You were totally dependent on your parents' choices. This dependence slowly sheds off as you grow into your teenage years.

Now you begin to make your own choices and do what you think is right. This is what taking the initiative is. Taking the initiative means making prior preparations to make good decisions.

It goes beyond just taking action. Taking the initiative is a life hack. You can apply it to everything you do — your business, your life, and even at home. Learn the power of taking the initiative, and you will be on top of every situation.

Why Is Taking the Initiative Important?

Taking the initiative will make you stand out from your colleagues as a good team player. It also makes you desirable for any job, as most employers appreciate it when you are proactive rather than reactive. Taking the initiative prevents you from making hasty decisions in your work, academic, and personal life.

When you take the initiative, other people will respect you and think of you as intelligent. It prevents avoidable obstacles from causing problems in your daily life. When you think ahead, you tackle issues that may arise and immediately address them before they become a significant problem.

Taking the initiative will also speed up your delivery of jobs or tasks. Once the obstacles have been addressed beforehand, your work will go smoothly.

How Can I Learn to Take the Initiative?

The following are tips you can use to learn how to take the initiative:

Be proactive

You have to always be prepared for anything. Do not let opportunities or problems catch you off guard. To achieve this, you must learn to look forward to the possibilities of things and how to get them done even before you are asked to do them.

Look at possible difficulties too, and think up early solutions to them. Use the knowledge you have at the moment to think of ideas and ways in which you can be a step ahead.

Ask for help

There is no crime in seeking help when you need it. Do not be afraid to do this. It is not shameful to admit that you do not know something. In fact, smart teens always ask questions and seek guidance from those who know what they don't know.

Voice your ideas

It is one thing to have initiative thoughts, and it is another to voice them out. You will only be seen as someone who takes the initiative when you voice out what you have in mind. You also build your confidence when you begin to share these initiative ideas at meetings or gatherings, as the case may be.

Take actions

This is more important in your personal life, where you make most of the decisions yourself. Be quick to take action. Don't wait for anyone to get things done for you. For instance, if you have an exam and know you are lagging in specific areas, seek help before it is too late. Always look for things that may set you back and tackle these before they transform into bigger problems.

Be Assertive

One reason teens are scared of taking the initiative is the fear of speaking up and being shut down. Confidence is important when you plan to take the initiative. Do not allow fear to draw you back. Instead, stand up for your beliefs, and don't be afraid to ask for what you want.

Prepare yourself for questions

You show how initiative you are in the way you react and your preparations to answer questions. When tasks are ahead, prepare for possible questions to be asked and also prepare answers for them. This will ensure you are not caught off-guard.

How Can Taking the Initiative Help You?

There are plenty of benefits to taking the initiative. First, when you take the lead, you are in control of your destiny. You are also more likely to get what you want because you are not waiting for someone else to give it to you.

It shows your drive and ambition, which can impress those around you. In addition, it shows that you are proactive and willing to take risks, and people see both of these as admirable qualities.

It can be frustrating when you feel like you are not being heard or your ideas are not going to the proper channels. But the truth is, the people around you want to be led by someone who is not afraid to go after what they want.

How do you start taking the initiative? It may not be easy, but it is achievable when you take the proper steps. Just remember these three essential things:

- Be proactive
- Offer solutions
- Take action

When you can nail all three of these, people will start to notice you. You will be on the path to achieving more extraordinary things in whatever line or place you find yourself in.

Exercise for taking initiative

Five things I need to take action on are:

1. _____

2. _____

3. _____

4. _____

5. _____

To take the initiative, I will start to...

_____

_____

_____

_____

_____

_____

_____

Five possible outcomes of my actions are:

_____

_____

_____

_____

_____

_____

What risks would I face if I tried to take the initiative?

_____

_____

_____

_____

_____

_____

What benefits would be available to me if I start taking action on important areas in my life?

_____

_____

_____

_____

_____

_____

_____

CHAPTER 5
PERSONAL DEVELOPMENT SKILLS

*"If you are under the impression you have already
perfected yourself, you will never rise to the heights you
are no doubt capable of."*

- Kazuo Ishiguro

Butterflies are so beautiful. They flutter their wings majestically and fly as though they were born that way. Who would have thought that a tiny larva would turn out to be such a beautiful creature? Butterflies go through different stages of growth to attain that level of perfection.

Like a butterfly, everyone must go through a stage to attain a certain level of success. So, likewise, personal development is your own stage of growth.

You participate in personal development whenever you actively work to improve yourself – for example, reading a self-help book, taking a course online, or even listening to a podcast.

Personal development involves gradually unveiling yourself until you completely understand who you are. Personal development skills are important for teens because they help them accept the changes around them and encourage them to develop into their best selves. It also gives them the skills and self-assurance they need to deal with any situation.

Self-Reliance

When you were a child, leaving your parents to make all the important decisions for you was easy. However, you had to rely on them for many things because you were too young to do them yourself.

As you grow into your teenage years, the narrative is changing. You are now old enough to know what interests and benefits you, and you should be able to make decisions based on that. Self-reliance helps you to do these easily.

Self-reliance is the ability to depend on yourself to get things done and trust your ability to meet your needs. It means you can do things and make decisions yourself without help.

As humans, we all need one another. So, it is normal to want to relate and interact with each other. It is also a good idea to take suggestions from your parents or more experienced people. But, remember that you should only do what is right in the end.

You might have close friends who are always there for you when you need them, but they won't always be. They, too, have lives to live, and you must respect that. Self-reliance will teach you to take control of your life. You will not be too dependent on others when you use this skill.

How Do I Become Self-Reliant?

You can become self-reliant by implementing the tips below:

Speak to your parents

Your parents have always had the final say in all of your decisions. So, at first, they might be reluctant to let you handle everything alone. Getting their trust is the first step to becoming self-reliant. It is easier for your parents to let you make your own decisions after you have earned their trust.

Tell your parents about your desires, goals, and decisions. They will be more trusting of you if you are honest with them. So, keep them up to date on what happens in your life; this will help to ease some of their fears.

By doing simple things like introducing your friends to your parents, calling to let them know where you are, and doing the right things even when they aren't looking, you can convince them that you can be trusted to make your own decisions.

Stick with your own decision

You can't claim to be self-reliant if you don't know how to

make the right decisions and stick with them no matter what. To successfully navigate your life as a self-reliant teen, it is essential to clearly define your priorities and outline the steps required to achieve them.

Your life will only be as good as the decisions you make. Therefore, you must learn to love yourself and make decisions that ultimately serve your best interests. You have to learn how to think well and make the proper decisions.

Get a job

It is difficult to make decisions and execute them when you do not have enough money to do what you want. Getting a job would not only allow you to have cash but will also keep you productive.

Do your chores

As a teenager, starting chores like cleaning the kitchen, taking out the trash, and organizing your room is essential to developing self-reliance. You will learn how to be responsible when you do these chores yourself.

You should also learn to cook for yourself. If you have to wait for someone to make meals for you at all times, you aren't fully self-reliant.

Go out

While it's still inevitable for you to live with your parents at this stage of your life, you need to get used to doing some things without them. For example, try going shopping, doing errands, and obtaining groceries without your parents' help.

Exercise for testing self-reliance

This worksheet will show how self-reliant you are. Tick yes or no for the questions below.

Question	Yes	No
Can I handle tasks when I am left alone?		
Do I do chores at home without being told?		
Do I shy away from leadership positions?		
Am I willing to do all it takes to achieve my goals?		
Are my choices easily influenced by others?		

Personal Finance (Budgeting and Money)

As a teen, you will be engaged in things that require money. For example, shopping for new clothing that will fit the changing shape your body will take. To do a lot of things, you will need money. Therefore, it may become a significant restriction if you don't have enough of it. Also, you would go cashless within a short time if you had money but lacked the skills to manage it well.

Everything you do as a teenager lays the foundation for what you will do as an adult. So, if you want to make enough money and manage it well, you must start learning how as a teen.

How to Earn Money As a Teen

Contrary to what a lot of people think, there are so many ways that teenagers can make money. You can be gifted cash by your parents, family members, or even friends. And ways you can earn money include:

Running errands

Your parents may require you to do errands for them, and they reward you with some cash. For example, they may ask you to go grocery shopping or take out the trash. They may decide to pay you for each errand you complete. If you own a bicycle, it would be easier to do this.

Pet Care

Pet care is a common service that people hire adults to do while away. If you charge a little bit less than the average rate for adults, you might be able to get more customers. Speak to your neighbors and friends about your love for pets and tell them about your rates. You can earn just by walking dogs.

Monetize your hobbies

One of the sweetest things to do is make money while doing something you enjoy. Monetizing your hobbies would make it easy for you to work and earn. You can get paid to sing at a party if you have a nice voice. If you love writing, then you can start a blog. You can do what you love and get paid for it.

Knowing how to manage the money you earn is very important. If you don't spend wisely, you will end up broke all over again. Borrowing will keep you in financial slavery. Instead, you should learn to save so you can pay for whatever you need. For instance, if you find a shirt you like, you can start saving up your money instead of getting a loan to pay for it immediately.

Budgeting is a good way to plan how you spend your money. A budget is a plan for the amount of money earned and spent over a specific period.

Budgeting Tips

Here are some tips for budgeting to get you going.

Determine how much money comes in

To have a good budget, you must be sure of the amount you would get at the end of a certain period. For teenagers, this could be regular cash from your job and money gifted to you on special occasions like holidays or birthdays.

Write out the necessary expenses

List all the important payments you have to make. They must include all those things you must consistently pay for as these are essential. For example, it could be your monthly cell phone bill or bus fare.

Practice your math

Once the necessary costs have been added, you can deduct that sum from your income. This shows how much you have left over after paying for your essentials.

Save up

After paying for basic expenses, what's left over should be put into your savings account.

Saving helps you prepare for the future. For instance, starting your business when you are older would be much easier if you start saving money as a teenager. You'll be better prepared to seize any opportunity that comes your way and will be able to avoid going broke in unforeseen circumstances.

The "fun stuff" can come in

You can now decide to spend on fun things. You deserve to enjoy yourself because you've worked hard. Buy concert tickets or go to the mall. These activities will reduce your tension and motivate you to work more.

Exercise for personal finance

Calculate your income

Source of Income	Amount earned
• Birthday gift from Aunt	$10
•	
•	
•	
•	
•	
Total	

Calculate your expenses

Expense	Amount to spend	Amount spent	Leftover
• Movies	$15	$12	$3
•			
•			
•			
•			
•			
Total			

Calcuate what is left

Total Income	Total Expenses	What's Left

What steps would you start taking to avoid spending extravagantly?

_____

_____

_____

_____

_____

_____

_____

Organization

Teenagers are a busy bunch, and life gets hectic during these years. One of the most important things you can do to help manage your day is to plan it. This way, you will know exactly what you have to do and when it has to be done, and you will have more time for other things.

How do I stay organized?

Although you have to juggle between school, extracurricular activities, assignments, and socials, finding a way to make positive use of your time is still important. Below are a few tips you would need to organize your day.

Get a Journal

A lot can be achieved when ideas are written down. You do not necessarily have to get the most expensive diary or journal. Just get a notebook and dedicate it to this. Then, the night before, write your plans for the next day and how you figure you'll achieve those plans. This will keep you current and prevent you from forgetting anything.

Prioritize

When planning your day, you should organize your plans in order of importance. Place the ones with higher importance at the top of your list, and others will follow. For example, is there a major thing you would love to accomplish that day? Then it should be at the top of your to-do list for the day.

Create a timetable

The major advantage of creating a timetable is that it makes you time-conscious. Set time frames for each task or goal as the case may be. This should take effect from when you wake up until you retire for the day. This will help you plan your day accordingly and avoid wasting time.

Set Realistic Goals

When planning, be sure to set realistic and feasible goals. You may not achieve anything on your to-do list if you set unrealistic goals. Aim for realistic goals and work toward achieving them.

Work with deadlines

It is important to set clear deadlines for every task so that you know when they're due. This gives you a feeling of urgency and reduces procrastination.

Go digital

We are in a modern world, where everything can now be done with the aid of technology. You can make use of some apps on your mobile phone to plan. Apps like planners, calendars, etc., can be used to track your appointments and events. This will help you stay on track and avoid conflicts or program crashes.

Set boundaries

One essential part of productivity is setting boundaries. Ensure you do not overspend, overwork, or overextend yourself. Set limits for various things. Social media, online gaming, naps, and other fun activities should have limited time. Flexibility is key when planning your day as sometimes unexpected things may happen. This will allow for the change in routine when necessary.

Be Optimistic

On some days, getting tired is inevitable. Don't allow this to kill your morale for that day. Get past it and keep moving. You will achieve more if you understand that mistakes are also part of the learning process.

It can be difficult to keep track of everything going on in your life as a teen. Still, you can manage your day more easily with proper organization and a productive strategy.

It takes time to get used to new routines. Do not rush yourself to get things done. Be patient. Being organized and productive does not happen overnight. You must put in the work to get your desired result. Just keep pushing ahead one step at a time. With consistency and determination, you will get there.

Things I Need to Do	How important is it on a scale of 1 to 5?
• Do my homework	5
•	
•	
•	
•	
•	
•	

Five things I will do to keep my room organized

1. _____

2. _____

3. _____

4. _____

5. _____

Dress Sense and Clothing Skills

Even if it sounds like a cliché, the saying *"As you dress, you shall be addressed"* is absolutely true. There aren't many genuine standards anymore when it comes to dressing properly. However, it's important to keep in mind that your favorite clothes aren't always the ideal options.

Nobody wants to appear like they are in their 50s when they're just sixteen. So, it is best to check all the rules below when selecting your clothes for an occasion.

Know your body type

When you know your body shape, picking out clothes that fit you isn't a problem. The dress that looks flattering on a slim girl might look uncomfortable on a girl with more skin. So even if you love a piece of clothing Beyoncé is wearing, you should consider whether your body type and size allow you to wear it comfortably.

Dress for the occasion

Most groups have that one person who dresses as though they're going to a prom date rather than a picnic. When picking out what clothes to wear, always consider the type of occasion you're going to.

Just pause to consider your plans for the day: will you be attending school or going to a party? The answer should influence whatever you're wearing that day. For example, if it's a sporting event, you shouldn't be wearing a tuxedo all day.

Be comfortable

It's best to wear comfortable clothes. Don't just wear what everyone else is wearing because it's trendy. Put on something that you want to wear, and when shopping for clothes, consider whether you will actually wear it or if it'll just take up space in your wardrobe.

Follow the rules

Imagine walking into a room full of boys wearing black shirts, and you are the only one wearing a white shirt. You will look and feel weird, right? That happens when you go to a function without checking the dressing rules. If there is a laid-down pattern or color code you should wear, you'd do well to abide by it. That will save you a lot of embarrassment.

Dress your age

When you were a kid, your clothes were made specifically for children. So, now that you have grown into a teen, you should stick with clothes meant for teenagers.

So many teens attempt to dress in a way that makes them appear much younger or older than they actually are. Attempting to wear clothes not intended for someone your age can make you look uncomfortable and out of place.

Exercise for Dress Sense

I feel comfortable when I wear clothes that...

_____

_____

_____

_____

_____

_____

When I am unsure of what to wear, I would ask...

_____

_____

_____

_____

_____

_____

_____

The color that makes me look my best is...

_____

_____

_____

_____

_____

_____

_____

The questions below will help you decide which clothes to wear.

Question	Yes	No
Does it fit my body?		
Is it easy to wash?		
Am I comfortable in it?		
Does it fit the occasion?		
Is it too trendy?		
Does it show too much skin?		
Do my accessories match it?		
Would I be able to wear it again?		
Is it my style?		
Can I wear it with other clothing items?		

Personal Grooming

Your body is changing; you're growing. So, washing your hands, brushing your teeth, and taking a daily shower won't be enough to keep you clean.

You may start noticing hair growing on a new body part. You might even start to sweat more than you normally do. These are normal changes that every teen goes through. You may be concerned or haven't gotten used to it yet, but I assure you it's nothing to worry about.

You'll need to learn more tips about keeping your body clean as you learn new things about your body.

Tips for Personal Grooming

The following are tips for personal growing:

Nail care

You will look neat if you keep your fingernails and toenails well-trimmed. Long nails often keep germs underneath them, so they look dirty and unattractive. Learn to keep your nails short and neat.

Biting your nails is a bad habit. You should cut your nails with clean nail clippers and not with your teeth.

Body Odor

You've always had sweat glands in your body. However, puberty makes these glands more active and releases more sweat, giving them a stronger smell. You could detect this smell under your arms.

Taking a bath twice daily with warm water and soap is the best way to stay clean. This will help to remove the bacteria that cause the odors. Keeping your skin and clothes dry and clean also removes germs and reduces strong body odor. In addition to keeping yourself clean, you can reduce body odor and sweat by using an antiperspirant or a deodorant.

Wearing clothes and underwear made of cotton or other natural materials may help absorb sweat more effectively if you sweat a lot.

Body Hair

Hair growth on the chin, upper lip, and pubic area is something that every teen faces. So, there is no need to be bothered when you notice it. However, you need to know when to trim or shave these hairs off to look clean.

You can shave using conventional razors, electric razors, soap, or other items. Never shave on dry skin; doing this can irritate your skin. Also, go slowly when shaving around a curved part of your body like your chin. If you move too quickly, you can cut yourself.

Dental Health

It is easier to interact with strangers and form friendships when you have a beautiful and healthy smile. A smile can make people fall in love with you without you saying a word. It can also increase your self-esteem and confidence.

If you don't take good care of your teeth, you could develop tooth problems that will make you feel uncomfortable. You need to brush your teeth at least once during the day and last thing at night. Brush for two minutes using a toothbrush with a medium-sized head and soft bristles. You could also care for your mouth by flossing and seeing the dentist regularly.

Smelly feet

The feet are the most neglected part of the body. If you do not want your feet to smell, you must take care of them just like you do for the other parts of the body. Give your feet extra care when you're taking your bath. Before putting on your socks and shoes, clean your feet thoroughly and ensure they are completely dry.

If your shoes are overly tight, there is a high possibility that your feet may become hotter and sweat more as a result.

You can reduce smelly feet by wearing shoes that are more comfortable or fit correctly. Also, change to cotton socks if you feel your current pair contributes to your foot odor.

Exercise for personal grooming

The questions below will reveal how intentional you are about grooming yourself.

Question	Yes	No
Do I brush my teeth before I go to sleep?		
Do I trim my fingernails and always keep them clean?		
Do I wash my hair frequently?		
Do I iron my clothes before I wear them?		
Do I have a deodorant?		
Do I bite off my fingernails?		

Staying Fit

Teenagers are energetic and constantly looking for ways to use their energy. They're hiking or sky diving if they are not riding a bicycle. These are ways you can effectively keep fit.

The human body changes and weakens as we age; this is a natural process. By staying fit, this aging process can be slowed down. It won't only help you stay healthy but it can also boost your mood and confidence.

Your teenage years are the best time to take your fitness journey seriously. You have all the time and strength to do that. However, you must make the most of it by staying active and engaging in sports.

What Does It Mean to Stay Fit?

To be fit is to be healthy. It means you exercise enough to maintain a healthy appearance and feel strong enough to carry out your everyday tasks and participate in simple sports.

Staying fit is the best thing you can do for your body during your teenage years.

How Can I Stay Fit?

The followings are effective ways to stay fit:

Regular Exercise
Regular exercise is one of the best ways to stay healthy and fit as a teenager. Every day, engage in exercises once you get out of bed. Regular morning jogs and climbing the stairs are all excellent options. Include them in your to-do list so that you don't skip exercising.

Exercises like these make you stronger and improve your mental well-being by releasing endorphins—chemicals that improve mood and pain relief.

Play a Sport
The football team I played in was a major part of my teenage years. I spent most evenings on the field with my friends. Most of my good friends are boys from that team. We got along so well during football games, and to date, we still speak to each other.

Playing a sport is a win-win situation. You have fun, meet new people, and also stay in shape. There are many sports to choose from. If you don't like going out, you could take up aerobic or weight training exercises in the comfort of your home.

Hit the Gym

The gym is the best place to go if you want professional and personalized training. You will be placed under fitness experts, who will give you exercises to engage in. As time goes on, you will begin to notice improvements in your physical and mental health.

Maintain a good diet

You are what you eat. If your menu is full of fresh vegetables and lots of water, you are careful with what you eat, and that's good. However, if your menu is full of junk, you aren't helping your body.

Stay away from over-processed and sugary foods. If you need to see a dietician, do it. Choose more fruits, vegetables, grains, and milk products. All these foods contain essential nutrients that help keep you healthy and fit.

Develop a good sleeping pattern

Anyone who wants to perform well at school or play their best in sports must get enough sleep. Sadly, a lot of teenagers don't get enough sleep. It has become a trend for teens to stay up late at night, watching movies and surfing the internet.

Sleep time is when the body gets to rest and rejuvenate itself. You should get at least seven to eight hours of sleep every night to be strong, energetic, and alert. Try to plan your time out and leave enough space for sleep.

Exercise for staying fit

What three activities do you do that help you stay fit?

1. _____

2. _____

3. _____

Eating Healthy

A box of chocolate, a can of soda, and a bowl of popcorn. This sounds like the perfect snack for a midnight movie. They taste too delicious to pass up, but they are bad for you.

It could be very difficult to control your cravings as a teen. There are different colors and flavors of junk foods to catch your attention. But this is when you must pay close attention to what you eat. The food you eat now will greatly affect your health later in life. Choose foods and beverages that are high in nutrients and low in added sugars, fat, and sodium.

How Can I Eat Healthily?

Here are ways to eat healthily:

Always eat breakfast

What happens in the morning can decide how the entire course of your day will go. It is the same way for food. If you start your morning with a healthy breakfast, you will feel positive and energized the whole day.

I grew up in a household that valued breakfast so much. Every morning, my family would sit at the table to enjoy breakfast before going about the day's activities. This not only helped us nourish our bodies, but it also helped us bond as a family.

Studies have shown that you should not skip breakfast. Eating a breakfast full of grains, oatmeal, or eggs will improve concentration. So, to be more active in school, you should not skip breakfast.

Fruits and veggies are your friends
The vitamins and minerals your body needs to flourish are abundant in fruits and vegetables. There are several fruits and vegetables available, and there are also numerous ways to serve them.

You can make a smoothie or blend fruit with yogurt if typical fruit or veggie salads taste boring to you. You could also dice different fruits and serve them colorfully.

Drink lots of water
I bet no one thought tasteless water would be so useful. Water keeps the body from getting dehydrated. You should consume at least 6 to 8 glasses of water each day. You'll notice that your skin will start to glow and feel stronger.

Stay away from soda
Psssh! That sound of a can of soda when you rip it open — it sounds like relief, but it isn't. Soda is bad for you. It causes your body to accumulate fat and may result in insomnia and anxiety since it contains added stimulants. Do not give in to the urge to pop open a soda; drink water when you get thirsty.

Exercise for eating healthy

Separate the healthy foods from the unhealthy ones.

Milk, Soda, Fish, Ice cream, Cakes, Vegetables, Eggs, Nuts, Potatoes, Chocolates, Candy

Healthy Foods	Unhealthy Foods

Hygiene and Cleanliness

One fond memory of my dad is how he used to mow our lawn. Seeing how beautiful the yard looked when he was done was pleasing. I also remember how my mum taught me to tidy up my room and fold my clothes when I did laundry. She ingrained cleanliness in me right from when I was young.

Many teens are so preoccupied with their social life, school, and other activities that they forget the importance of hygiene and cleanliness. You are gradually becoming responsible for everything around you. It is not too early to start taking care of your space.

Hygiene and cleanliness are very important not only to teens but to others around them too. However, your hygiene is incomplete if it does not extend to your environment.

How Can I Maintain Hygiene and Cleanliness?

You can maintain hygiene and cleanliness by doing the following:

Keep your kitchen clean

The most sensitive part of the house is the kitchen. This is where your food is prepared. So, it needs to be squeaky clean. Trust me, many things can go wrong if your kitchen is messy. Keep your kitchen clean so you can eat healthily.

Take out your trash can every day. This will keep your kitchen from smelling of rotten food products. Also, wash napkins after use and keep all pots and plates in designated positions.

Wash your hands regularly

Every child needs to be taught the importance of hand washing. Once you learn to always wash your hands as a kid, keeping up when you become a teenager won't be difficult.

Your hands are the gateway into your body's systems. If you eat with dirty hands, you stand a chance of taking in bacteria through your mouth. Touching your eyes with dirty hands could cause eye infections too.

Keep your toilets clean

Most parents agree that their kids avoid cleaning the restroom. But whether you like it or not, mastering the art of bathroom cleaning is a skill that is important for hygienic reasons.

You should learn how to properly clean the toilet to prevent bacteria and bad odors from thriving in your house.

Do regular cleaning

I discovered that if I didn't clean up my room when it was still a bit untidy, I always felt too overwhelmed to get anything done. Clean your space regularly. Do not wait till your house is a complete mess before you clean it up. As frequently as possible, move around and give attention where it is needed.

Exercise for personal hygiene

What are some good hygiene habits that you have?

_____

_____

_____

_____

_____

_____

_____

_____

What have others said about your hygiene?

_____

_____

_____

_____

_____

_____

_____

What changes would you make to improve your hygiene?

_____

_____

_____

_____

_____

_____

_____

Cooking and Food Skills

This is a survival skill that every teen should learn. Soon enough, you'll be living on your own, going to college, or having your own family, and you'll need to learn how to make your own meals. So, it would be beneficial to pick up the cooking skills that will come in handy.

One reason why learning to cook is useful is because you know exactly what goes into your meal. You can ensure the hygiene of the ingredients and cooking utensils you use. You can choose your ingredients while keeping your preferences and allergies in mind. But, again, this is something that a restaurant might not do for you. You could also pick up cooking as your hobby for the rest of your life.

Some Important Cooking and Food Tips

Here are some important cooking and food tips:

Go grocery shopping
Grocery shopping is the first step in learning how to cook. However, before you go to the store, it's important to make a list of the products you need to buy to keep to a budget. I buy many unnecessary items whenever I go grocery shopping without a list. Setting up a budget can prevent wasting money on things you don't need.

Keep an eye out for the expiry dates of food products when shopping. The product may become harmful if expired; its flavor, color, or texture could also change.

Wash all ingredients and utensils properly
Ensure all counters, kitchen utensils, and cutting boards are

clean before you begin cooking. Wash all raw ingredients thoroughly before you put them in your meal. To prevent the spread of bacteria, don't let raw meat, fish, or vegetables come into contact with other foods that are ready to eat.

Learn how to cook basic meals

Several dishes are both easy to prepare and healthy. Some examples are omelets, scrambled eggs, grilled cheese, baked vegetables, and soups. In addition, you can look through the numerous recipes available online.

Find different recipes to cook based on the types of things you enjoy eating. Eggs, rice, spaghetti, tacos, salads, simple soups, and chicken are just a few useful foods. They can serve as the basis for many different dishes.

Use your measuring cups

Measuring cups and spoons are the most accurate equipment to use in the kitchen. They are useful when you want to measure uncountable ingredients. You should use a measuring spoon rather than guessing the amount of salt, sugar, or oil needed in a recipe. You can also buy a food scale if you can afford it. If you can't, you can still do fine without one.

Keep your cooking space clean

Any leftover food scraps should be thrown away. Next, clean the stovetop and counters with a detergent, and wash any cutting boards or other utensils you used to prepare the food. After handling raw foods like chicken and beef, always wash your hands and any surface the raw food has come in contact with.

After cooking, putting out the trash can daily is advisable. By doing this, microorganisms from the garbage can will be kept out of your kitchen.

Exercise for cooking and food skills

What are your favorite foods?

_____

_____

_____

_____

_____

_____

_____

Write out what recipes you would like to try out. Tick it when you do

Recipe		Recipe	
• Pasta	✓	•	
•		•	
•		•	
•		•	
•		•	
•		•	

Whether it's your parents' day off or you just want to cook on your own, you can try out this easy, no-fuss recipe to cook a delicious breakfast.

Vegetable Omelet with Toasted Bread

This yummy vegetable omelet filled with fluffy egg is an easy go-to breakfast recipe that you can cook yourself.

Ingredients:

- Half chopped onion
- One egg (whisked)
- One-half tomato, thinly diced
- Two tablespoons of boiled corn
- One-half bell pepper, thinly sliced
- Half a tablespoon of sesame seed oil
- Half a teaspoon of mixed dry herbs
- A handful of chopped baby spinach
- One teaspoon of mixed shredded cheese

How to make it:

- Add all the ingredients into a bowl (except the cheese), and whisk properly with a whisker or fork.

- Set the bowl aside.

- Heat oil over medium heat in a skillet.

- When the oil is warm, add the egg mixture to the skillet and cook until both sides look golden brown.

- Transfer the egg to a plate and serve with toasted whole grain bread. As a side, you could add boiled snap beans and mashed potatoes.

Personal Healthcare and Basic First Aids

Health, they say, is wealth. Hence, you need to pay close attention to your health. Having a healthy lifestyle is by no means an easy task. You need a lot of discipline and self-control to get through it. Nevertheless, you can develop a personal health care routine to improve your overall well-being.

As a teen, your health determines how much work you can do. If you are ill, you won't be able to go to school or do anything else. These easy health routines would make it easy to live a healthy lifestyle.

Basic Health Care Routines for Teens

Regular exercise
You feel your raw strength and abilities manifest themselves during your teenage years. You become more sensitive, stronger, and alert. Exercise helps to bring all these into shape.

Exercise makes your memory sharp and also improves brain functionality. When you exercise from time to time, you are likely to have better grades in school. This is because exercise improves memory, so retaining everything you've read and studied is easier.

Exercise also increases concentration and aids physical fitness. Teens are expected to exercise for at least one hour per day. However, you don't necessarily need to go to the gym to begin your exercise routine. Dancing, long walks, running, and biking are simple exercises you can engage in as a teenager.

Have a quality sleep
You need about 8 to 10 hours of sleep daily to function your

best during the day. Sleep helps you recover all the energy lost during the day's activities. It also helps your brain rejuvenate. Your sleeping hours are as important as your sleeping time. Your sleeping time is when you lie in your bed as you transition into a sleeping state, while your sleeping hours are the hours you spend sleeping. The best time to sleep is usually between 9 pm and 11 pm.

Limit your screen time and have a sleep diary as a healthy sleep routine. Inside the diary, you can record your time of sleep every day. Additionally, you can write an overview of your day and a preview of the following day's tasks. Doing this ensures that you go into bed with a clear mind.

Don't abuse drugs

Drug abuse is a societal disease. But, unfortunately, it is increasingly popular, especially among teenagers. Common drugs teens abuse include cocaine, opioids, inhalants, and others.

Generally, low self-esteem, depression, shock from traumatic events, and anxiety are major factors that cause the abuse of drugs among teens.

Drug abuse exposes you to a lot of mental and physical disorders. As a result, you risk developing a heart attack, stroke, kidney and lung damage, and many other unplanned outcomes.

In your teenage years, you take on more physical activity. You can trip and fall from running and playing with your friends and perhaps develop a cold or any other form of sickness at any point. So, you need to familiarize yourself with basic first aid tips in these situations.

Basic First Aid Tips for Teens

Here are some first aid tips you can keep handy:

Wounds, cuts, and bruises

- For wounds and cuts, the first thing you should do is rinse the wound surface.
- Apply pressure to stop the bleeding.
- Apply methylated spirit to kill bacteria lurking around the wound surface.
- Cover the wound with a clean cloth or bandage.

Fever

When you notice you have a fever with a high temperature, do the following;

- Take a bath to reduce your body's temperature.
- If you are feeling chilly, cover yourself with a blanket.
- Drink enough water or fluids to stay hydrated.
- Take a pain reliever.

Exercise for personal healthcare

Tick all that you have in your first aid box

• Scissors		• Tweezers	
• Bandage		• Safety pin	
• Pain relievers		• Gloves	
• Gauze		• Antiseptic	
• Splint		• Cotton swab	

CHAPTER 6
EMOTIONAL AND SOCIAL SKILLS

Emotional and social skills help us connect and interact with one another, including the use of gestures and body language. These skills are necessary regardless of the situation — whether chatting with an online friend, assisting a complete stranger who needs directions, or even speaking with a grocery store attendant.

These skills are displayed in various ways. For example, it could be when you smile to make someone feel welcome, refrain from making hurtful remarks, or observe someone's body language to infer their mood. You use these skills when you pause to consider how your actions or words can influence others.

I have a friend who loves to travel. He goes around the world and meets people from diverse cultures. My friend once told me about his experience in an African country. In this place, kneeling was a normal way to greet people. People would kneel or bow to an older person when saying hello.

They weren't bothered by it because they were used to it. My friend had to adjust to this culture for the duration of his stay. However, he kindly spoke to them and showed no bias against their way of life.

During your teens, you will go to places you never thought you would. You will have to interact with a wide range of people, most of whom will have cultures or habits that you consider weird. Emotional and social skills will help you interact and relate well with them despite your differences.

Emotional skills are necessary for teens to know how to treat each other with respect, kindness, and decency. Any teenager who has these skills will be able to communicate well. This would, in turn, help them to grow and sustain healthy relationships with others.

Examples of emotional and social skills include:

Listening

A smart teen is one who can listen well. All other skills in this book won't help you much if you cannot train yourself to listen well. Listening skills are skills that everyone needs. You cannot avoid them at school, at home, or in the world.

Unfortunately, most teenagers don't know how to listen properly. It's not entirely their fault, though. They grew up thinking that listening means zoning out for a little while and then joining the conversation again. A good listener must listen to understand rather than just respond to what the other person is saying. You must also learn to keep your thoughts to yourself unless asked.

Knowing what not to say when it is your turn to speak is another important component of being a good listener.

How Can You Become a Good Listener?

Here is how you can become a good listener:

Listen closely

To be a good listener, you need to concentrate fully on what is being said. Listening carefully will help you know what the speaker is saying and how to respond correctly.

Stay away from distractions of any kind. It could be your phone, a noisy toddler, or a music source; put away anything that can distract you and focus solely on what the speaker is saying.

Make eye contact

There are many reasons why some teens avoid looking others in the eye. They might be shy or don't know how to do it. Avoiding eye contact can imply that you are uninterested in what the speaker is saying.

A general rule that could help is to hold eye contact 50% of the time when you're talking and 70% of the time when listening. Also, do not stare at the speaker for too long; it can make you look creepy. Try to maintain eye contact for at least five to ten seconds. Then take a few seconds to casually glance to the side before making eye contact again.

Read body language and facial expressions

Body language is something you don't say out loud but express with your body movements, postures, and facial expressions. These can reveal a lot about what you feel.

You need to understand how to read others' body language and know how much your body language speaks for you too. Recognizing this will help you understand people better. When listening to someone, ensure that your body language does not signal to the speaker that you are uninterested.

Exercise for listening skills

This table shows how good your listening skills are.

Question	Yes	No
Do I try to interrupt when someone speaks to me?		
Do I wait or pause before asking for clarification?		
Do I make eye contact during conversations?		
Do I listen to understand the speaker?		
Do I try to note the speaker's important points?		
Am I easily distracted during conversations?		
Do I give off the right body language?		

An example of a time when I wasn't really listening and how it could have gone differently if I had been listening is...

_____

_____

_____

_____

_____

_____

What do other people have to say about my listening skills?

_____

_____

_____

_____

_____

_____

_____

What would I start doing to ensure that I improve my listening skills?

_____

_____

_____

_____

_____

_____

_____

Making a Good First Impression

Do you know that it typically takes someone three to seven seconds to create an opinion of you once they first meet you? People will quickly judge you based on your appearance, body language, attitudes, mood, and clothes. An impression is formed immediately, and it might be difficult to change it.

Nowadays, people have very short attention spans. Therefore, they will not be all over you for too long. So, you must know how to catch their attention within the first few seconds of meeting them.

First impressions may not mean much when you're with close friends, but when you start your first job or go to college, you will depend on them more than ever.

How Can You Make a Good First Impression?

Before I share tips on making a good impression, I want to clarify this: making a good first impression doesn't suggest that you pretend or change who you are to please someone else. Instead, it means you choose to show your best side and true self when you meet someone new. A great way to create a good first impression is to make other people comfortable and feel good in your presence.

That said, here are tips you can use to ensure you are remembered the right way:

Dress well

When you walk into a room, your clothes are the first thing anyone will notice. From your appearance, people will be able to tell if you are a decent person. Your dress sense would speak for you before saying anything. This is why you have to always look your best.

Paying attention to the details of your outfit will not only make you win the hearts of people around you, but it will also make you feel confident. Make sure you wear clean clothes that fit your body shape.

Greet with a smile and a handshake

You should start by being cheerful and courteous. It would be rude to walk past people without saying "hi." Smiling is a great way to ease tension. When you smile, you come across as approachable, and this will help to create stronger bonds with others. Smiling will also help you feel good about yourself.

Different cultures have different ways of greeting. But generally, a smile should be followed by a firm handshake.

Not everyone is a hugger, so hugging might come across as intrusive.

When in doubt about how formal to be when addressing someone, stay on the side of formality. It is better to come across as extremely professional than to assume more cordiality than the other person is comfortable with.

Compliment the other person

Giving compliments is a very effective way to make people feel at ease. It would go a long way in making people willing to speak to you. This does not imply that you should lavish people with false praises just to get into their good favor. Simply look for something you really like in that person. It can be their smile, a lovely watch, or a perfectly ironed dress. That casual compliment can act as a good way to start a conversation.

Just be yourself

People around you can always tell when you're trying to be someone you're not. If being funny or playful doesn't come naturally to you, don't try to force it. Be yourself and maintain your normal demeanor; your personality will attract the kind of people it should.

Make connections

If you feel like the person you just met will make a good friend, ask for their phone number and arrange to meet up with them later. For example, you could invite them to lunch or take them on tour around your neighborhood. You can also send a follow-up text or email to say how great it was to meet them.

Exercise for making a good first impression

Tick "P" (positive) for the good impressions and "N" (negative) for the bad impressions

	P	N
Chapped fingernails		
Rumpled clothes		
A warm smile		
Skimpy clothes		
Trimmed haircut		
Slouched posture		
Nice deodorant		
Grumpy face		
Firm handshake		

Empathy

Have you ever felt horrible because someone else is struggling or in pain? That is empathy at work.

One Sunday afternoon, my brother and I were playing a game in the sitting room. He was running around while I tried to catch him. I failed to catch him after three attempts before finally succeeding on my fourth try.

He tried to escape while I held the hem of his shirt. I yanked him back with force as he tried to get away. When I eventually decided to let go of him, he landed on the ground.

I didn't expect that to happen, so I screamed in fear. I was probably more worried than he was. I felt bad I had let that happen, and I consoled him. That was empathy in play. Empathy is what makes us human.

Empathy means imagining yourself in someone's place so that you can feel their pain. It is the ability to relate to the emotions or experiences of another person by envisioning what it's like to be in that person's position. You express empathy when you share emotions with another person, even when you are not directly responsible for their predicament.

You could also show empathy by trying to understand another person's perspective on a problem, even if yours is different. Empathy allows you to put your own perspective on a situation aside and consider how someone else might be feeling from their perspective.

How Can You Build Empathy?

Empathy can be learned by:

Listening closely

Empathy starts when you decide to listen to emotions.

When your best friend calls you and needs to vent about how terrible she feels since her breakup or how stressful school has been, you need to listen. You will understand how the other person is feeling if you listen well.

You have to be sensitive enough not to interrupt when a vulnerable person speaks to you. If you are just thinking about how you can express your own feelings during a conversation, then maybe you aren't listening to what the other person is saying.

Your ability to understand and empathize with others will improve if you make an effort to actively listen when people speak. Learn to be conscious of the cues others give off that may reveal their mood. For instance, let's assume your friend is sad about his grades. He might be reluctant to come straight out and tell you he's sad. However, empathy will make you notice the change in his actions.

When someone shares their feelings with you, take advantage of the chance to relate and be open with them. Spend time actively listening to them so you can get their perspectives without jumping to conclusions. If they need encouragement, you can talk about a time when you experienced emotions that were similar to theirs. It would show that you really care.

Do not judge

Every human has a tendency to judge others. It takes a conscious effort to avoid condemning people, especially if they are the cause of what they are going through.

We all have stereotypes typically focused on color, gender, and age. These stereotypes reduce our ability to empathize because they give false impressions, influencing how we react. These stereotypes also reduce our willingness to try to understand someone with different experiences or cultures. It takes time, practice, and exposure to people to develop the ability to live with empathy in your heart.

You become more empathetic when you learn to stop criticizing or judging others for their mistakes and decisions.

Learn new things

It might be difficult to empathize with someone when you don't know enough about them. Knowing more about people and their lifestyles will make it easier for you to put yourself in their shoes when needed.

Start by getting to know other people's lifestyles. For example, read books and articles written by people from various backgrounds or initiate a conversation with a stranger. You can build your empathy by being curious about people outside your immediate social group, being open with them, and getting to know them.

Take action

Know that you can influence someone else's life in some way, no matter how small the effort you put in. Showing your love and concern is great, but why not take it a notch higher by doing something that will make the situation easier to bear?

Many people value it when you do things to make them feel loved. With this in mind, after speaking love to people in pain, take action to make the situation more bearable.

Exercise for practicing empathy

In the table below, write out what emotion is felt and how you would react to each situation.

Situation	Emotion	Reaction
Your classmate lost her pen.	Sadness	I would console her and lend her my spare pen.
Your neighbor just got a new cat.		
Your brother hit his toe against a stone.		

Your dad got drenched by the rain.		
Someone on the news won a medal.		
Your best friend got a bad grade in math.		

Behavioral Skills

As you grow, you realize that some skills are necessary to develop yourself. In contrast, other talents are needed to improve your interaction with your friends. The set of skills that you need to help you relate well with others is called behavioral skills.

Behavioral skills are abilities that determine how productive you will be, how you interact with others, and your response to situations. These skills influence your thought system, emotions, and actions. When you develop behavioral skills, you begin to think, act, and respond better to situations.

These skills also help to improve your social relationship. This means that they enhance your ability to bond with your friends. In addition, developing behavioral skills will help you communicate and associate well with your peers.

Examples of behavioral skills include the following:

- Decision-making
- Time-management
- Communication

- Empathy
- Stress management
- Patience
- Problem-solving
- Balance
- Healthy living
- Emotional intelligence
- Risk-taking

How Can Behavioral Skills Benefit You?

Some teens often find it difficult to interact with their peers. It may be that they lack confidence or feel inferior. Developing behavioral skills, especially communication, can help.

You improve your quality of life by developing communication skills, empathy, patience, healthy living habits, and many other qualities. Consequently, as you transition into adulthood, you become more responsible, mature, organized, and you are a better individual.

How Can You Develop Behavioral Skills?

With the following tips, you can utilize your behavioral skills and succeed through stress management, effective interactions, and consistent effort.

Choose a behavioral skill

There is a wide range of behavioral skills you can learn and build. The first step is to focus on one that you think would be most useful for you. This might prove to be a difficult task because they are all very good options. Nevertheless, you must relax and understand that taking one step after the other would be the best option.

Some skills might not fit into what you really need at the moment. So, consider some factors in choosing the right skill. These factors include your temperament, time, and purpose.

To choose the right behavioral skill for you, do the following:

- Observe your temperament and personality.
- Note the behavioral skills that come to you naturally.
- Develop your natural behavioral skills.
- Make a list of the ones you'd like to learn.
- Match the list to fit your temperament.

Practice the skill

You'll probably hear this saying throughout high school, "Practice makes perfect." After choosing a behavioral skill, practice comes next. It is the most important part of building any skill. For example, you should take on tasks to practice your problem-solving skills. Not tasks that will be an uphill battle for you to finish — take on tasks that are worth the stress. While you're at it, find innovative solutions to complete this task. This will improve your problem-solving skills.

Always schedule your activities if you need to improve your time management skills. For example, you probably have found yourself in a situation where you have to do your assignment, run an errand, read for a test, and prepare for school the next day. To begin with, set a deadline for each and all of the tasks. Then proceed to execute the tasks within the timeframe you've set.

Set short-term goals

Slow and steady wins the race. To build and master a behavioral skill, you need to set short-term goals to track your learning efficiency. Don't try to handle everything all at once. Instead, break up long-term goals into small ones, mark them after you've reached the targets, and continue your learning process.

For instance, if you are working on your communication skills, you can set a short-term goal of initiating conversations among your friends. While at it, you can assess how well you can engage them in conversations.

Setting short-term goals will help you to monitor your progress. It will also boost your confidence in building your behavioral skills.

Observe and learn from others

There is always someone out there who has done something you aim to do. Other people have already exhibited the behavioral skill you want to build.

Take your time, observe the people around you, and learn from them. Then, as you build your skill, observe those people and notice how they implement these skills in their day-to-day activities. For example, you can observe your class representative for stress management traits. Note how he can manage his academics with his other class responsibilities.

Also, you can look to your parents or guardians for decision-making and problem-solving skills. Parents have a lot of decisions to make every day. The list is endless, from repairs or replacements at home to the choice of food to make. So, you should pay attention to them and observe how they approach and make these decisions.

Track your progress

After your skill has taken root in you, track your progress. But, of course, to track your progress, you have to observe your results. When you begin using your behavioral skills, the results will show how well you have progressed in your learning.

You might need to practice more in some cases. Also, after you have mastered a skill, you can learn another. Then, simply repeat the outlined process.

Exercise for behavioral skills

The good behavioral skills that I showed today are...

_____

_____

_____

_____

_____

_____

Poor behaviors that I showed today are...

_____

_____

_____

_____

_____

_____

How did these behaviors affect me today?

Positive Behaviors	Negative Behaviors

What behavioral skills do I want to learn tomorrow?

_____

_____

_____

_____

_____

What would I do to make sure that I achieve these goals?

_____

_____

_____

_____

_____

Coping with "Negative" Emotions (Mental Health)

Emotions are very powerful. Most teens react and make decisions based on the emotion they feel at the time. This is why learning how to cope with certain emotions is necessary.

There are many ups and downs in life. There will be times when you feel good. You laugh out loud, dance, and scream with joy. However, there will also be difficult times when you feel gloomy and wish you were left alone. Negative emotions cause a lot of problems for teens. They could lead to other bad experiences if not properly handled.

Everyone feels gloomy once in a while. Unfortunately, you just can't help it sometimes. It may be tough, but you can develop the skills to deal with negative emotions.

How Can You Cope With Negative Emotions?

Feeling sad or gloomy is not a bad thing. It is natural to feel that way sometimes. In fact, some negative emotions could push you to do better when done rightly.

Negative emotions become harmful only when you spend most of your time sulking about how bad you feel; when they begin to affect how you relate with others. It might be tough to deal with negative feelings, especially when you're a teenager. However, the following tips will help you deal with such feelings without developing unhealthy habits.

Identify what you feel
Most times, you don't understand what you feel. You have a feeling, but you're not sure what it is. When you name your emotions, you not only start to understand what is upsetting

you, but you also start to discover how and why you feel bad about it. You may feel better as a result of that clarity.

It is much easier to eliminate negative emotions when you know what you are after. Learn to put a name to whatever you feel. Putting those emotions into words reduces their intensity a great deal. For instance, if you are mad because your friend spoiled your backpack, just say it. "I am angry with my friend for ruining my backpack."

Finding out what you feel lets your emotions healthily run their course. It also makes it easier to experience relief from it.

Talk about it

Communicating your feelings has a way of making you feel better. Tell someone how you feel. If no one is within reach, then journal. Whenever I am upset, I write down my feelings in my journal. I always journal why I feel upset and how I plan to get over it. I also read some affirmations to myself to feel better.

Don't repress your emotions. It is much better to acknowledge the emotion and tell someone about it than to try to hide it or lose control. Talking about why you feel that way would help ease your emotions.

Ask yourself why you feel that way. For instance, why do you feel angry that your friend ruined your backpack? Instead, you could say, "I feel angry now that my backpack is ruined because now I have nowhere to put my books."

Think positive thoughts

You will need to change your thoughts to positive ones. If you don't, you can lose your thoughts and focus on how awful everything is. This would, in turn, make you feel much worse.

You might not feel like it at the time but try to do the things that make you happy. For example, let's assume you just lost someone important to you. You might not want any company at the moment. But going out with friends can help you overcome that negative feeling.

Make it a habit to acknowledge and concentrate on all the positive aspects of your life, no matter how small they may be.

You need time

It will take some time before you are fully back to yourself. Do not let anyone force your feelings out if you aren't ready. You will not suddenly jolt out of a bad mood — you will need time to get better, and you should do it at your own pace.

Even with all your efforts, some tough emotions might still be impossible to get through on your own. You should seek additional support if your feelings of sadness last for more than a few days or if you feel so angry that you start thinking of harming yourself or others.

Speak with your parents, school counselors, or a therapist about how you feel. Therapists and counselors have received training in helping people learn how to overcome negative emotions. So, they can provide you with a ton of advice and suggestions that will kick you out of your gloomy mood.

Exercise for coping with negative emotions

What emotions do you struggle with the most?

_____

_____

_____

_____

_____

_____

_____

_____

How will you cope with these emotions?

Emotions	What I would do
When I am angry, I will	
When I am scared, I will	
When I get jealous, I will	
When I am sad, I will	
When I feel tired, I will	
When I get worried, I will	
When I feel irritated, I will	
When I feel inferior, I will	

Tick "Yes" for the right ways to deal with negative emotions and "No" for the wrong ways to deal with them

What should you do?	Yes	No
Talk about your feelings to a good friend		
Scream in anger		
Take deep breaths		
Say positive affirmations		
Beat up your sibling		
Skip school		
Speak rudely to everyone		

Making Meaningful Conversations

Naturally, teens have a flair for starting conversations with others. You might be an introvert, but you would still be able to start a conversation with your friend when you are together. While conversing with people, you must be careful about what you discuss.

Not all conversations are beneficial. Some conversations can tamper with your thought process, and some can make you change your life for the better. Thus, it is not a matter of how long a conversation is but how helpful and meaningful it is. Unfortunately, not everyone understands what meaningful conversations are, let alone how to start them.

Meaningful conversations are discussions that can positively influence your life or the listener's life. But why are these kinds of conversations important to you? It's quite simple. Teenagers are one of the most vulnerable groups of people. They can be easily convinced and influenced by their friends and other people.

Most teens listen to and learn from their friends more than they heed their parents. Instead, they prefer to study and imitate their mates. And this is why neurologists describe the teen phase period of brain development as a *"learning phase."*

How will a meaningful conversation benefit you?

Having meaningful conversations with your friends is important to your well-being. When you have a deep conversation with someone, you feel a sense of acceptance and connection with the person. This will make you feel understood and refreshed. In cases where you feel anxious or depressed, a good conversation with someone might be what you need to overcome a bad mood.

In addition, having meaningful conversations aids your self-growth and development. You will be amazed at how much you can learn from others. You'll learn many life lessons, from talking about careers to lifestyle and academics. If you have the right ideas and practical suggestions to offer, even adults can learn from you.

How can you make meaningful conversations?

Every skill can be learned. It might take a while, but you'll become a master at it. Having meaningful conversations isn't any different. Here's all you need to make good contributions to a conversation.

Listen and be attentive

Listening is perhaps the most important part of a conversation. Relax; show that you are listening with your body and mind. People will be more inclined to give you more information if you are attentive. Being a good listener will improve the quality of your conversations.

Try to see things from each other's perspective

You need to communicate and connect freely with your peers. One of the best ways to do this is to engage in interesting, meaningful conversations. However, it is important to note that a conversation between you and your friend can go wrong if one of you gets the wrong picture of what the other is saying.

Your friend will stop a discussion when they feel they are not understood. In case you're in this same situation with someone who suddenly stops talking to you, there's something you can do about it.

One perfect trick to understanding a person's statements is to imagine yourself in a similar condition as that person. Once you do this, you'll be able to interpret each part of the statement. Thus, even if the speaker is a stranger, it's only a matter of time before you connect well and emerge as good talking partners.

Ask deep questions

At times, being inquisitive is a great way to sustain a conversation with a person. There are a lot of ways you can introduce questions into your discussions. For instance, teens love discussing career or lifestyle topics.

During a career discussion, you can ask deep questions about each other's goals and pursuits. For example, ask about the higher institutions you're aspiring to and the courses you wish to study. During conversations like this, you'll discover people with goals that are similar to yours.

Conversations that involve asking deep questions are good ways to learn more about each other and build good relationships with friends.

Be natural

Don't pretend; just be you. Let the conversation flow naturally. Don't try to be who you are not to impress the other person. Instead, maintain your identity and share your opinion confidently. Perhaps, try to gain a common ground between you and the person.

Don't force a conversation on something you don't know about. Instead, simply tell the other party you don't have enough information about the topic. You will appear fake and pretentious if you pretend to know something you don't.

Not everyone will like you for who you are, and that's okay. People are entitled to their own opinions and thoughts. Nobody's opinion is more important than yours, and yours is no more important than that of someone else. To build a meaningful conversation, you have to be yourself. Do not hesitate to give your honest opinions.

Have a good sense of humor

It is very normal for conversations to get boring sometimes. In this case, having a sense of humor is a good way to lighten the mood. You don't have to force a joke — that could make you feel awkward. Instead, understand where the conversation is going and when you can crack a joke. Make sure the joke is appropriate and as light as possible.

Sometimes your body language will do the trick. You just have to know when to use that. This is very important when starting a conversation with a stranger. For example, making them laugh when necessary will help them relax and be more open to continuing their conversation with you.

Exercise for making meaningful conversations

What are some topics that interest you?

1. _____

2. _____

3. _____

4. _____

5. _____

6. _____

List some meaningful topics you can coin out of your topics of interest.

1. _____

2. _____

3. _____

4. _____

5. _____

6. _____

Describe a time when having a meaningful conversation has helped you.

_____

_____

_____

_____

_____

_____

_____

Taking Feedback

Knowing that some people think poorly of your efforts could be very painful. But you should know that nobody is perfect!

No matter how hard you try, you will still make mistakes, and people will have to let you know what to work on to prevent the recurrence of the mistake. This is why you must learn how to receive feedback.

Nobody likes giving advice to someone they know won't take it seriously or who might take offense and overreact. However, learning to accept feedback with honesty and an open mind can build trust with people and help you experience constant growth.

How Can You Take Feedback in the Right Way?

While it may be easy to accept feedback personally, it is important to strive to see feedback as an opportunity to learn and improve. Taking feedback the right way can reinforce your current strengths, clarify the effects of your behavior, ensure your directed behaviors are on course, and boost your ability to detect and find solutions to your errors. The following tips will help you receive feedback and handle it correctly.

Listen respectfully

You need to set aside the pain in your heart and listen to the speaker's words. If you begin the conversation expecting the speaker to say something that will offend you, then even a compliment would sound like an attack. The speaker won't be able to properly convey their point of view to you.

Ask questions

If you are unsure of what was said, ask questions. Make sure you and the speaker are on the same page. One helpful tip is to repeat what the person has said to you. Making notes would also help you remember all that was said. Use open, friendly body language and gestures to engage and demonstrate that you are paying attention to what the speaker is saying.

Appreciate the speaker

Remember that if someone agrees to give you feedback, they

might be willing to continue supporting you. You have to appreciate them for paying attention to notice your mistakes.

Showing gratitude means that you appreciate the speaker's contribution to your project. It also keeps you in their good books. Thank the giver for being willing to provide honest and courteous criticism.

Don't argue or be defensive

Arguing with someone because they gave you honest feedback shows that you do not value growth. On the other hand, if you become defensive, it shows that you never cared all along about what the speaker said.

It is okay to make a few clarifications here and there when you're being misunderstood. But, taking things too seriously and turning them into a fight tells others that you are not willing to get better. So, do not make hasty rebuttals until you completely understand what the comments mean.

Work on improvement

Start acting after you identify the crucial areas that need improvement in your feedback. Sharing it with the people who gave you the feedback will show that you are acting on their advice. They might even come up with suggestions you hadn't thought of.

Exercise for taking feedback

In your opinion, did you handle your tasks well? What could you have done better?

_____

_____

_____

_____

_____

_____

_____

What did others have to say about the way you handled your task?

_____

_____

_____

_____

_____

_____

_____

How did you feel when you were given feedback?

_____

_____

_____

_____

_____

_____

_____

Do you honestly feel that the feedback given to you was right?

_____

_____

_____

_____

_____

_____

_____

How do you plan to handle your tasks better next time?

_____

_____

_____

_____

_____

_____

_____

_____

Basic Manners

Many parents teach their teenagers good manners in their childhood. But some teens throw away all these manners because they want to look cool and bougie in front of their friends. Having good manners will benefit you in many ways. It shows that you have respect for other people and for yourself too.

Whether speaking with someone, going out with friends, or meeting someone for the first time, showing good manners will always come in handy. Teens who behave well will definitely be respected more.

Nobody wants to be around someone who isn't courteous, so showing good manners will attract good people to you. As a result, you will be able to make more friends and build better relationships with people.

People are always happy to be around courteous people. Friends are more likely to enjoy each other's company when they respect others and behave politely. You will feel confident, perform better in school, and generally live a happier life when you show good manners.

Basic Manners You Should Know Are:

- Make sure you apologize when you have done something wrong.
- Don't use slang when speaking with someone new.
- Do not touch other people's belongings without asking for permission.
- Don't answer phone calls when you're in a conversation with someone. If it's an urgent call, then excuse yourself.
- When speaking to someone, maintain decent eye contact with the person.
- Be polite. Learn to say "please" and "thank you."
- Don't grab things out of other people's hands.
- Say "excuse me" when you need to interrupt a conversation or when you accidentally bump into someone.
- Do not litter the streets.
- Don't be grumpy.
- Be polite when engaging people online. Do not make offensive comments.
- When you are meeting someone for the first time, stick to handshakes.
- Make sure you cover your mouth and nose with your elbow when you have to sneeze and cough.
- Don't put out too much personal information online.
- When dining, observe excellent table manners.
- Never send someone unsolicited texts or pictures.

- Be patient and wait your turn when conversing with others.
- Avoid shouting or replying angrily to insults or snide remarks.
- Be kind to service providers. For example, don't be impolite to cleaners or speak down to cashiers.
- Don't post pictures of others without their permission.
- Keep devices off the dining table.
- Chew with your mouth closed.
- Offer to help others when you can.
- Own up to your faults.
- Be positive.

Exercise for basic manners

Separate the good manners from the bad manners

> *Eating loudly; Saying "excuse me"; Using curse words in public; Throwing paper onto the street; Flushing the toilet after use; Shouting in public places; Obeying traffic rules; Fighting; Obeying people in authority.*

Good Manners	Bad Manners

FINAL WORDS

Life skills are necessary for every stage you enter. Life can be tough and filled with challenges, but with life skills, you can prepare yourself and navigate with experience. This book aims to equip you with the tools you'll need to build resilience and live a fulfilled life. Therefore, it is essential to start learning them early. Teens need to learn to prepare for adulthood early, just as toddlers start learning motor skills early too.

Before we end this journey, I'll like to leave you with a few tips you can use to learn life skills.

- Choose wisely; you can start with tasks you are interested in before moving on to those you struggle with.

- You can ask for help from your parents. Tell them to show you how to tackle a task to make it easier for you to model.

- Look for opportunities that will show your needs for specific skills. Your needs can lead to more learning. For example, you may not be interested in learning how to change a car tire until you are stranded at the roadside with a flat tire. Looking for opportunities will push you to be more receptive to mastering life skills.

You need life skills to function daily as they are essential to thriving in the real world. Knowing that many of these skills aren't taught in school, and teens without the knowledge struggle to find themselves out there, I've written this life-skills guide to teach most of the skills teens need to survive and thrive.

This book has discussed 35+ essential life skills teens need to win in the real world. The aim is to make adulthood easier. If you've read to this point, you should be ready to take on anything!

Whether you are heading off to college, still in high school, or already in the real world, I hope you've had a great read and learned a lot to make adulthood easier.

So far, you've learned:

- What are life skills, and why do you need them?
- Business skills
- Universal skills
- Entrepreneurial skills
- Emotional and social skills
- Personal development skills

I believe this book has provided you with practical, simple, and real-world advice that you can easily employ to win in the real world.

Before I close, I recommend you to read our other books in the series. These books are written especially for teens and their parents. You'll find them very helpful. The details are given on the following pages.

Best of luck!

The Mentor Bucket

Book - 2

Life Skills for Tweens Workbook

Essential Life Skills Every Pre-Teen Needs but Doesn't Learn in School

How to Cook, Clean, Solve Problems, and Develop Self-Esteem, Confidence, and More

---

INTRODUCTION

Hey, kiddo!

How prepared are you for the world out there? Do you think you are well-equipped with essential life skills that make it easy to transition to your teen years and adulthood? Can you look after yourself if left alone for a while?

Of course, kids grow up quickly. Before you know it, your 8-year-old self is already a 16-year-old, driving off in your first car. Oh well, even if it won't go that fast, you can't deny that with the advancement of technology and media growth today, many things seem to be happening faster than we had imagined. So, it shouldn't be surprising.

You must have heard stories of the highly intelligent boy who can't find his way around budgeting and, as a result, is winding up in debt. Perhaps you've also heard about the good students struggling with living on their own as they start college. Or the professional who allows people to talk down to them because they don't know how to stand up for themselves.

What do you think these three people have in common? The answer is simple—they lack some essential life skills that would've helped them navigate life better and become successful in what they do.

Many parents tend to focus on academics alone and forget about teaching their kids basic life skills that are important to their success, such as managing money, doing their laundry, and building their self-confidence. Without these life skills, many educated people will still find themselves struggling in the workplace and life in general.

While you may be able to acquire certain life skills in school, some essential ones aren't taught. So, the need for this book!

Learning isn't all about finding out how to spell and mastering the timetables. There's a lot that happens outside the classroom that you need to know. This book will teach you 25+ important life skills you need; what they are and how to practice them. Learning these will set you up for the future.

With the life skills you'll learn in this book, you will develop the right foundation for your personality, with enhanced positive traits. You will become independent, and you'll be able to function without supervision.

Every parent wants their kids to grow up and stand on their feet without much help from mommy and daddy. Even though the day you become independent is still many years away, you can start building your independence and mastering the skills and strategies you'll need later in life.

The life skills you're about to learn in this book will give you an idea of what you want to do in life and the kind of person you want to be. We're about to focus on educating you in a way you'll find fun and exciting.

Now buckle up, and let's get started!

CHAPTER 1
THE BASICS OF LIFE SKILLS

If I gave you a plain sheet of paper, what would you write on it? Would you write a beautiful story or draw a colorful picture of JJ from Cocomelon? Whatever you decide to do with the paper determines what the paper becomes.

This is how life is. It's like a plain sheet of paper on which nothing is written. Only you can decide what you need to write on this paper. If you want your life to turn out beautifully, you need the right life skills to make that possible.

Life skills are very important at this stage of your life. You need them to help you grow into a respectable and responsible adult. You need life skills that enable you to live in peace with yourself and others. It'll help you discover yourself and work toward becoming the best version of yourself.

We all need life skills. Your mom, dad, siblings, and friends need them to survive. Nobody can navigate life properly without having the necessary life skills. Even animals need them. For example, how would a lion survive in the forest if it couldn't hunt for prey? Hunting is a lion's life skill.

So, what is your life skill? Is it cooking, cleaning, or talking? Let's find out.

Here's an exercise to help you find out the life skills you already have.

Exercise: Things I do every day...

I...	Yes	No
Ex. Cook food	✓	
Help do the dishes		
Tidy up my room		
Talk to my friends with confidence		
Ask random questions		

Exercise daily		
Do things without wasting time		
Save money		
Make good choices		

The Value of Life Skills

You go to school to learn math, science, and other subjects, but not life skills. Life skills aren't mandatory for being taught in classrooms, even though they're important and we can learn them from our family and personal experiences.

Many kids your age don't understand the value of life skills till they're grown. They don't understand how such simple activities will help them live better. But it can be simple. Life skills are a part of our everyday life; we need them to really experience life beautifully.

If you learn life skills now, you're more likely to be happier and more confident later in life. Learning life skills will help you succeed in your studies, career, and personal life! You'll learn and grow confidently—ready for life as an adult!

If you learn these skills, you'll do terrific, even when your parents and friends aren't there to give you support.

Exercise: Match each life skill in the left column with the activity in the right column that might come from it.

Life Skill	Activities
Cleaning skills	Speaking to people in an audible, polite way
Cooking skills	Being confident in yourself
Money management skills	Going to school early
Communication skills	Preparing breakfast
Time management skills	Saving up money
Personal development skills	Washing plates when you're done eating

Why Are Life Skills Important for Tweens?

Imagine that you have a beautiful pen. All your friends love your pen so much that they want to have it too. But there's a problem. Your pen stopped working. When you put your pen on paper and move your hand to write, it does nothing. Would you still love the pen the same way? Would you throw it away because it's useless?

This shows how important life skills are for kids like you. Life skills are essential for you to be useful for yourself and society. You can discover your true self and be your best version with life skills.

If you don't have life skills, you won't be comfortable where you find yourself. It's difficult to survive if left without a guardian. Life skills make it easy to connect with others and make new friends even in places you've never been.

Exercise: Things I can do without help

I can	Yes	No
Brush my teeth without help		
Put the trash in the right place		
Make choices on my own		
Tidy my room		
Use good manners		
Follow simple instructions		

Parents' Role in Teaching Life Skills

When you were a baby, you didn't know how to walk, brush your teeth, or comb your hair. But as you grew up, your parents taught you to clean up, read, write, and do other things.

You meet your parents first when you are born. They're the ones you look up to—to guide and protect you. They stay with you when you cry and give you what you need to grow well. You trust your parents' decisions because you believe they know better. You adopt their lifestyle and behavior as yours because you don't know any other way.

I couldn't do many things for myself when I was a little boy. I didn't know how to tidy up my room or keep my clothes clean. I just wanted to play football or have fun with my toys.

My parents taught me everything I knew. They made me understand that life is more than playing football and watching cartoons. My mom and dad taught me how to clean, arrange my clothes, and speak to people politely.

Kids follow their parent's behavior and actions. Therefore, parents have an important role in pushing their kids to learn life skills. A child that learns life skills from their parents is more likely to be happy, healthy, and willing to learn.

Exercise: Some good behaviors I have learned from my parents are...

Ex. Saving my money

_____

_____

_____

_____

_____

_____

_____

_____

CHAPTER 2
DOMESTIC SKILLS

I remember that I didn't like helping out with home chores when I was younger. I used to run away and pretend to be sick anytime I was asked to do the dishes or clean up the kitchen counter.

My mom always said that chores were not just for girls. She'd talk about how important it was for me to help around the house. And to ensure that my sister and I didn't end up fighting, she'd share the work to be done equally between us.

Domestic skills are skills we use at home. They make life easier for you and others around you. No one is born with domestic skills. Instead, we learn them. As a tween, you should help out around the house. You make life easy for yourself, your mom, and your dad when you do your chores well. For example, your mom could have had a very busy day at work, and you helping her out with a few chores could make her feel better.

I remember when I got into college, every domestic skill I learned at home became very useful for me. It was easy to clean up my room and cook meals for myself. I did it happily. In fact, everyone called me a chef, but I really wasn't one. I was just a young boy who picked up cooking skills from helping in the kitchen.

You can bond with your family over chores. It'll be fun to tell your mom how your day went while helping her in the kitchen. And your dad would be so happy to see you laughing at his jokes while you help him wash the car or trim the flowers.

Some domestic skills you need are:

Cleaning

You may have many toys, books, clothes, hair accessories, and more. You must learn to keep your belongings clean and tidy. Your room is your personal space, and you spend most of your time in it. So, it's only right that you clean your room.

Before you go out every day, clean up any mess you made the previous day. Make your bed neatly and pick the dirty clothes and toys up off the floor. If you share a room with anyone, make sure you work together to ensure your room is always tidy. For example, you could suggest the parts of the room you'll clean and make your sibling handle the other parts. Sharing duties with your siblings makes it easier to complete your tasks. In addition, it helps you know what to do and when to do it.

If you decide to clean the house, you might choose to clean the yard, porch, and living room. Then, your siblings could do the dishes and clean the kitchen. This way, everyone is working on getting the job done more quickly.

Get rid of torn clothes, and don't hold on to old toys so your room doesn't get filled up with things you don't need. As you sort your belongings, be sure to throw away any papers or books that aren't useful.

Cards, books, letters, toys, and other keepsakes could be kept on a shelf or in a box such as a storage container. Your clean clothes should be neatly folded in the box or hung in your wardrobe. Dirty clothes should be put away in a laundry bag. Shoes are meant for shoe racks. Then, the stationery should always be in the stationery box. Never leave a pen or pencil lying carelessly on the table or floor. Also, don't leave snack wrappings or fruit peelings lying around the house. Pick them up.

Don't wait for your parents to yell at you before you clean up the house. Instead, take up responsibilities without being told. Do whatever chore you're told to do, and don't waste time when doing it.

If you're the oldest child in the house, be an example to your younger siblings. Show the other kids what to do. Younger ones usually follow what the oldest does. So, let them learn from your actions.

If you're having difficulty keeping up with cleaning your space, you can draw up a cleaning checklist. The checklist is a list of all chores that need to be done. It helps you arrange your chores well. You can use the checklist below to keep yourself on track.

Exercise: Things I have done

I have...	✔
Folded my clothes	
Done the dishes	
Vacuumed the floor	
Dusted the shelves	
Thrown old clothes and toys away	
Emptied the trash can	
Made my bed	
Put my toys away	
Arranged my shoes	

Write your other tasks here and put in a tick mark once they're completed

Ex. I have put the shoes on the shoe rack	✔

Exercise: Things I need to do daily, weekly, and monthly

Every day, I'll...	Every week, I'll...	Every month, I'll...
Make my bed	Change my bed sheets	Arrange my clothes
Put my toys away	Take out the trash can	Throw out torn books and broken toys
Clear out my desk	Dust the shelves	Decorate my room
Put dirty clothes in the laundry basket	Wash my dirty clothes	Clean under my bed
Put garbage in the trash can	Vacuum the floor	Declutter my room

Cooking

Have you tried cooking on your own? Did it turn out to be a nice meal or a horrible disaster? Was it fun for you, or do you think it was boring? If you don't know how to cook, that's not a problem. There are lots of grownups as well who can't cook! But if you want to become an adult who can live on their own, eat healthily, and spend wisely, you need to learn how to cook.

No one can live without food. A hungry kid is a grumpy kid; grumpy kids don't get anything done. You don't need to cook a big, five-course meal. You can start by making toast or boiled eggs. Start with simple, safe utensils and cooking methods.

The quickest way to learn to cook is by watching others do it. You'll watch closely what is being done with each meal. You can also help out in the kitchen when meals are being prepared. Help to cut up veggies, measure out or peel ingredients, stir ingredients, and do other things that will make the meal prep easier.

After the stress of the week, your parents deserve a break, don't you agree? A Friday night off from cooking duty would be such a big relief for them. Of course, there'll be adult supervision. But there's nothing as relaxing as sitting back and letting others do the cooking.

The weekend is perfect for practicing the meals you watched your mom or dad prepare. They should be there to guide you.

The first time I was on cooking duty, I felt so happy. My mom permitted me to do it, and I promised not to burn down the house. The meal wasn't so tasty, but it wasn't bad either. Looking back now, I know my mom told me that it was delicious, just to encourage me. I wasn't concerned about how it tasted. I was just happy to have the family eat something I made.

While helping out in the kitchen, you might discover a passion for cooking. You can start forging a career in cooking, and you might just be our next big chef, right?

Exercise: Things to know before you start cooking

I can...	Yes	No
Identify herbs and spices		
Use the rice cooker with supervision		
Cook over a stovetop with supervision		
Slice and dice vegetables		
Use measuring cups and spoons		
List ingredients used in cooking		
Operate blenders and other food processors		
Handle sharp utensils like knives and forks without supervision		
Turn the stove off and on		
Pack my own lunch		
Identify tastes and flavors in food		
Stir batter in a bowl		

Exercise: Which kitchen practices are safe and which are not safe?

Activities	Safe	Not Safe
Rolling up your sleeves before cooking	✓	
Tying your hair back (for girls or boys with long hair)		
Reaching over the stove when it's on		
Throwing knives and spoons around		
Playing with fire		
Washing your hands before cooking		
Handling hot utensils with your bare hands		
Adding too much spice to food		

Laundry

No kid should smell like dried sweat or the ketchup from last night's dinner. This is why doing laundry is important for you. You need to look and smell fresh. But most importantly, doing your laundry helps you eliminate the germs from dirty clothes.

Wearing clean clothes daily feels like a good idea until you have a pile of clothes to wash. Well, do you have a choice? You have to wear clothes daily, so there's also always laundry to do.

I was 10 years old when I began doing my laundry. I started with little things like my socks and underpants. I once tried to wash bigger clothes but did it badly. I didn't sort the clothes, so I'd put both dark and light clothes together. Guess what? My clothes got ruined. The colors of the dark clothes bled and ruined the lighter-colored clothes.

My mom was furious because just one mistake had ruined so many clothes. She told me to always ask for assistance when I wanted to wash clothes and taught me how to sort my clothes before washing them.

Laundry doesn't have to be a bore. Here are some tips to make doing laundry easier and more satisfying for you.

Sort the clothes

Sorting is the most interesting part of doing laundry. It means grouping clothes together according to their color and the type of fabric they're made of. You have to separate all colored clothes from white and darker clothes.

You can put all the red clothes in a basket, all the white clothes in a bowl, and all the brown clothes in your laundry bag. Sorting your clothes ensures that the colors from the dark clothes don't stain the lighter colors as they're being washed.

Sorting is also when you turn the clothes inside out, if necessary. Always read the label for any instructions on how to handle the fabric.

Check for stains

If your clothes have tough stains, you might need to pre-treat them before washing them. You can't do all this alone, so you should ask adults for help. You'll avoid many mistakes if you ask for help when you aren't sure what to do.

Put the clothes in the washing machine
Put the clothes of similar colors together and, with the help of an adult, load them into the washing machine. You should also choose the right detergent for your clothes.

Although this might seem the simplest idea, you must be careful. Ensure you don't overfill the washing machine with clothes. Use the right amount of soap and other washing liquid. If you use too little, the clothes won't get clean, and if you use too much, it becomes hard to rinse the soap out of your clothes.

After washing and rinsing, you can load the clothes into the dryer and then take them to the folding area. Always wait for an adult's supervision before you handle the washer or dryer.

Put the clean clothes away
When you've washed and dried the clothes, put them in the right place. All your efforts will go to waste if you keep your clean clothes on a chair in your room or in a dirty box.

Clean clothes should be hung in wardrobes or folded and put into drawers. Do not leave clean clothes all over the place.

Exercise: Items I need for my laundry are...

Dirty clothes	✓	Knives	
Forks		Pots	
Phone		Washing machine	
Dryer		Detergent	
Washing liquid		Water	

Bed		Dog	
Dirty socks		Sticks	

Exercise: Things I would do before doing my laundry

I will...	Yes	No
Ask for guidance from an adult	✓	
Put too much washing liquid in the washing machine		
Wash colored clothes differently		
Turn the clothes inside out		
Overload the washing machine		
Switch the washing machine on and off without any reason		
Sort out my clothes before washing them		

Grocery Shopping

As you grow older, you won't always have your mom and dad by your side. So, you'll have to get things done without them. You'll have to clean and cook for yourself. Grocery shopping will play a large part.

Grocery shopping is a great way to train yourself to spend money wisely and become aware of your essential needs. So, whenever you see your mom or dad going grocery shopping, ask to tag along.

Tagging along would teach you to know your way around the store. For example, you know what aisle has canned goods, frozen foods, or dry grains. You also learn about the prices of food and how that changes.

The tips below will help you enjoy grocery shopping.

Have a shopping list

A grocery list is where you write out what you need to buy so you don't leave anything out. It also teaches you to budget well. So the next time an adult makes a grocery list, pay close attention to what is written and ask questions about what you don't understand.

Check for the ingredients you already have at home so you don't buy what you don't need. Also, buy the ingredients you need for the week. For instance, there's no point buying pasta if you won't be eating it till next month.

Check expiry dates

No one knows how long those groceries have been on the shelves. So, checking for expiry dates before paying for food items is best. Spoiled or expired food is bad for you. Even if it looks fine, don't buy it.

Put groceries where they should be

Grocery shopping doesn't end when you buy the groceries. It ends when you put these groceries where they should be. Whenever I didn't go grocery shopping with my mom, I'd be the first to help sort them out when she got home. I knew the canned foods would be taken to the pantry and the meat to the freezer. Milk, cream, and eggs should be in the fridge.

I'd carefully arrange them in their respective places. I didn't even need anyone to explain where they had to go because I had always watched mom arrange groceries.

Exercise: Find the words in the box.

Chicken, Carrot, Orange, Coffee, Soda, Salt, Rice, Pasta, Sugar, Sauce

J	F	V	S	U	G	A	R
C	B	C	J	I	T	D	P
O	W	H	S	D	E	Y	A
F	S	I	R	E	I	O	S
F	A	C	A	R	R	O	T
E	U	K	I	I	A	R	A
E	C	E	O	C	Y	A	Z
O	E	N	P	E	D	N	A
S	A	L	T	O	X	G	Y
H	Z	K	S	M	N	E	G

Cleanliness and Hygiene

Now is the time to learn proper hygiene if you haven't already been taught. You need to learn how to wear clean clothes, cover your mouth when you cough, and trim your nails.

Good hygiene habits are formed over time. These skills start forming when you're a baby and stick with you for the rest of your life. If you don't want to keep getting sick, you must keep yourself and everything around you clean. Good hygiene and cleanliness help you feel good about yourself. You will feel comfortable with other people if your clothes smell and look nice. Your friends will also love and respect you more.

In your tween years, you're very active. You want to stay outdoors all day and play with your friends. You return home all sweaty and sticky. Do you scrub your body in the shower after hours of play? Do you trim your nails when they get long? Do you change your underpants regularly?

Here are some ways to maintain good hygiene:

Wash your hands
Since you were in elementary school, nursery rhymes have told you about how washing your hands and brushing your teeth can help you stay healthy. These rhymes train you to become healthy and responsible adults later in life.

We touch millions of particles of dirt and dust every minute. So, we must make hand-washing a habit. Washing your hands keeps germs away. Wash your hands thoroughly with soap and water whenever you use the toilet. If you can't find soap and water, keep a hand sanitizer in your backpack and take it wherever you go. You can get rid of germs on your hands with just a few drops.

Take your bath every day

If you wash your body regularly, especially after playing with your friends, you can get rid of the dirt on your skin. A bath would also wash away sweat that might cause a bad smell.

You must bathe every morning after you wake up and just before you sleep at night. You should never go to bed without having a bath. You can choose a body spray with a nice fragrance and spray it on your body after having a bath. It'll help you feel and smell good.

Change your underwear every day

Your underwear is closest to your skin, so it can transfer germs to your skin and cause an infection if it is carrying bacteria. This is why changing your underwear and other clothes is very important. There are so many germs on dirty clothes.

A kid that wears dirty underpants will eventually smell bad. You shouldn't wear underwear more than once without washing it. Keep all your underwear clean and dry.

Brush your teeth

There are tiny germs in your foods and sweets. When these germs stay in your mouth without being cleaned with toothpaste and a toothbrush, your mouth begins to smell.

I doubt anyone wants to be friends with someone who has a smelly mouth. So you must learn to brush your teeth twice every day. If you feel pain in your teeth, talk to an adult about it so you can see a dentist.

Care for your hair

Your hair is also a part of your body. Unfortunately, many kids ignore their hair and leave it messy. This is bad. Get a new haircut or ask your parents to get your hair done whenever your hair is too full and rough. Ensure you wash your hair regularly. If you cannot wash your hair by yourself, ask for mom or dad's help. Proper hair care prevents itchy scalps and lice. It also makes your hair shine.

Don't bite your fingernails

Your hands are everywhere and are exposed to dirt. Ensure you take care that they stay clean. If you have to trim your nails, use a nail cutter. Biting your nails is a bad habit. Besides allowing germs into your body, it makes your nails look ugly.

Exercise: Some good hygiene habits I have are...

Ex. Taking my bath twice a day

_____

_____

_____

_____

_____

_____

_____

_____

Exercise: Things I do

Do I...	Yes	No
Take a bath every day		
Clip my fingernails and toenails with a nail cutter		
Cover my mouth when I cough		
Wash my hands frequently		
Brush my teeth every day		
Take good care of my hair		

CHAPTER 3
KNOW THE VALUE OF MONEY

Let me guess—you've wasted money on things you don't need at times, right? Does your mom keep all your money because she knows you'd spend it foolishly? Do you want to get a better grip on your spending habits?

Let's be honest—every kid wants the best toys. You want to buy clothes, favorite snacks, cakes, and cotton candy. You'd be very happy if you had them. But, you also don't want to be penniless. You want to have some money left in case you want to do something else later. You want to grow into an adult that spends money wisely.

There's nothing wrong with spending your money. It only becomes bad when you start spending too much. Think of how much you spend on candy in a day. Don't you think it's too much? Also, consider how often you spend money buying pizza or burgers with your friends after school. It's a huge amount when you sum it up. So why not throw all that money into your piggy bank and save for something better?

When I realized I was a huge spender, I got a clear piggy bank and saved money in it every day. Every time I bought candy, I had to put money in the piggy bank too. I watched my money go from $2 to $20. That made me happy.

Before, I'd spend all my money recklessly because I thought more would always come. I didn't know my parents had to work hard to get money. I thought they just needed to go into the bank and request a huge bag of money.

Think about your clothes and shoes, haircut, and books. Your parents need money to pay for them. Do you know how much these cost? If your parents just bought cotton candy and ice cream with their money, they wouldn't have enough money to pay for your education or meals.

To fully understand the importance of money, you need to pay for some things yourself. Maybe volunteer to pay for something small, such as a seasoning pack, anytime your mom goes grocery shopping.

Exercise: Setting a spending limit

Setting a spending limit helps you control how much money you spend. A spending limit is the highest amount you allow yourself to spend in a day. Let's say I set my spending limit at $10 every day. I can decide to buy anything I want if its sum doesn't exceed $10.

In this exercise, quickly fill out what you'll do when you have spent your money and when you save your money.

If I spend all my money...	If I save my money...
Ex. I'll be left with nothing	I'll have a lot of money to do better things

My spending limit for this week is...

Sun	Mon	Tues	Wed	Thurs	Fri	Sat
Ex. $10						

Learn How to Save

Saving is an excellent way to manage money. It means spending less than you get. For example, let's assume that you have $10. If you decide to spend $5 and keep the other half, you have saved it.

Saving means putting away some money to do something else instead of spending it on things you don't really need. Saving trains kids to become adults who can plan for the future and achieve their financial goals.

You can ask your parents to help open a kid's bank account that pays interest to see how money stays safe at the bank and how it will increase over time.

Your parents give you the basic things to live comfortably, but you might need to sort other things out yourself. For instance, instead of asking your dad for a ball and a doll, you can save up to buy the ball yourself and let daddy get you the doll. You could also save up to pay for movie tickets, jewelry, books, or birthday gifts for friends.

You don't have to spend money just because you have it. Instead, learn to always save some money for emergencies.

The following tips will make saving easy for you.

- **Start small and increase bit by bit**
  You can start by saving at least a penny every day. Then, you can increase it to two pennies or more as time goes on. Set aside part of your allowance and put it in your piggy bank. This saves you the headache of asking for money when you need cash urgently.

- Don't buy things you don't need
  If you can go a day without something, don't buy it. Know the difference between wants and needs. Your needs are things you can't live without, like food and water. Your wants are those things you can live without, like ice cream and cupcakes.

  Saving makes you a smart shopper. You buy what you need, not what is trending.

- Have saving goals
  You are not too young to set saving goals. Spending all your money is easy when you don't have goals attached to your spending. Saving goals are things you save up for. Let's say you save up to buy a nice shirt. Then buying the shirt is your goal.

- Keep your savings safe
  Don't just keep your money in your pocket, books, or bed. Instead, keep it in a piggy bank where you can easily access it, or ask your parents to help you create a savings account with a bank.

Exercise: Saving and spending checklist

I would spend money on...	I would save up for...
Ex. Fruits	Movie tickets

Write out some good money habits and bad money habits you know.

Good money habits	Bad money habits
Buying only what I need	Spending all my money at the mall

Here's a checklist to track the money you've saved up.

I'm saving up to buy		The total amount I need is
On the...	I saved...	I have a total of...
2nd of June	$5	$5
3rd of June	$7	$12

Balance a Checkbook

Balancing a checkbook means checking your financial records to ensure they are accurate. It shows that you've recorded each transaction—the amounts entering and leaving your bank's checking account.

If a store charges your parents the wrong amount for a purchase, they may not know initially, but they will find out when balancing their checkbook. Learning how to balance a checkbook will be very useful when you start working and earning money. It can help you track your spending habits, make budgeting easy, and identify mistakes in calculation.

Kids should know how to make a simple budget or balance a checkbook before they become teens. You should start taking financial lessons on checkbooks and budgeting. This way, you train yourself to become a responsible financial leader when you're older.

So, how do you balance a checkbook? It can be a piece of cake. However, to do it correctly, you must follow these tips:

- Always write down the total of all purchases in a notepad when you go grocery shopping.

- Write out deposits and withdrawals from the bank (income and expenses). Then subtract the sum of all purchases from the available balance in the account (the money left).

- Always go with your parents to the store.

- Once you've practiced balancing a checkbook a few times, you can discuss it with your parents. Let them check what you've done and correct your mistakes. Ensure you understand how it works.

Sometimes, your checkbook just doesn't get balanced. What do you do then? Check your records again and see where the mistakes are. Maybe you forgot to record a particular transaction or have mixed up some numbers. Go back and check it carefully from the beginning. This way, you'll find where the mistakes are.

Modern Ways of Balancing your Checkbook

Few people use pen and paper to balance their checkbooks these days. It's an old practice.

Using a pen and paper to balance your checkbook is stressful, and you're more prone to forget the numbers and make mistakes.

You can now balance your checkbook properly by:

- Online banking
  With online banking, you can see your money as it is at any time, any day. You can even check your balance, send and receive money, and pay for things. If you spot errors, notify the bank immediately to get them corrected.

- Use a spreadsheet
  Your cell phone or computer is the fastest and easiest way to balance your checkbook on the go. You can create a spreadsheet on your phone for easy reference. Spreadsheets let you enter your daily, weekly, or monthly transactions. You don't need to draw a table; it's already there for you.

- Use an Account Aggregator App

An account aggregator app is easy to use. It monitors and records all your funds and does all the hard work for you. You just need to compare it with your daily transactions to ensure everything is equal.

Exercise: Balance your checkbook here

Check	Date	Transaction	Deposit	Withdrawal	Balance
567abc	June 27th	Birthday Cake	$300	$200	$100

Use the information in your checkbook above to fill in the boxes below.

What do you spend the most money on?	
Do you deposit more money or withdraw more money?	
Do you spend more on your needs than on your wants?	
Where do you get most of your money?	
Do you think you have good money habits?	

Understand Bill Payment

Bill payments are necessary for the house you live in, the clothes you wear, the food you eat, and so on. We pay bills for almost everything! Learning about bill payment teaches you to take responsibility for your finances and pay invoices when they're due.

The urge to spend money increases as you get older. You'll want to buy flashy and beautiful things, but make sure that you've paid all your bills and saved before you start throwing money around.

A key part of financial education is learning how to pay bills, save money, and stay out of debt. You're on your way to financial stability if you can balance all three.

Most kids don't know how everyday objects and activities are connected to bills.

You can ask your parents to choose one or more things that involve money. Then, ask them to identify the bills. For example, a rental payment is for a home, and a cell phone payment is for data or phone usage. This way, you'll learn how bills directly affect your money.

Exercise: Match the items in the left column to their bills in the right column.

Car		Cable bill
Television		Water bill
House		Rent
Internet		Gas/ Insurance bill
Water		Electricity bill
Electric cooker		Electricity bill

Write out some items you would like to pay for.

I can pay for...

Ex. A pack of salt

_____

_____

_____

_____

_____

_____

_____

_____

_____

CHAPTER 4
PERSONAL DEVELOPMENT

Growing up doesn't only mean adding a year to your age. It comes with changes to your body and mind. As you grow, you'll learn things like lacing your boots efficiently and buttoning your shirt properly. But it doesn't end there. You'll also learn about yourself and discover what you like and don't like.

As you grow, you must learn personal development to become a better person. Personal development means knowing yourself and taking steps to get better. It helps you understand who you are and what you can do. It also drives you to focus more on what you're good at.

Not only does personal development help you become better, but it also makes you relate with other tweens well. It helps you focus on your good habits and your work toward changing bad habits.

When I was 10 years old, I became aware of myself. Before then, I was doing what every other person thought was good. I didn't really know what I wanted. A few days after my tenth birthday, I started discovering myself. I picked up a journal my dad gave me as a gift and wrote down everything I knew about myself. I wrote about things I loved about myself and the things I needed to change. You can try it out too.

I love...	• Ex. Reading comic books • •
I don't like...	• Ex. Partying • •

I love myself because...	• Ex. I'm kind to others • •
I'm good at...	• Ex. Playing the guitar • •
My favorite thing to do is...	• Ex. Play with my pet • •
Sometimes I need help with...	• Ex. Getting my homework done • •
When I am older, I want to be...	• Ex. A writer • •
I want to learn how to...	• Ex. Bake chocolate cake • •

My family says I'm...	• Ex. Cheerful • •
My friends say I'm...	• Ex. Funny • •
I say I'm...	• Ex. Awesome • •

This fun exercise exposed me to things I never knew. I found things I was terrible at and things I loved doing. I also discovered that I loved musical instruments. So I asked my parents to get me a guitar as a birthday gift the next year, and this marked the start of my love for music.

This exercise was my little way of trying to get better. Because I wrote down how terrible I was at cleaning my room, I started working toward keeping my room tidy. And I was successful at it. My mom even told me how much I had improved.

Personal development made me learn about myself and take responsibility for my actions. The things I learned stuck with me throughout my tween and teenage years and made me a better adult.

Be Accountable

'I didn't do my chores because I have homework."

"I forgot to water the flowers because my sister distracted me."

Do these statements sound familiar? If they do, that doesn't sound good. It's the voice of a lazy tween, blaming someone else. When you make mistakes, do you accept corrections or put the blame on someone else?

Being accountable means doing things assigned to you and taking responsibility for the results they bring. When you're accountable, you don't blame others for your mistakes. Instead, you accept that you make them and seek ways to prevent them from happening again.

My parents taught me how to be accountable when I was very young. They assigned tasks that I had to do every day. They wrote these tasks on paper, and we'd check out all I had done at the end of each day.

If I completed all my tasks, I got an extra candy, but if I didn't, I wouldn't be allowed to watch TV. This made me feel responsible for something in the household.

My sister had her tasks too. For example, I had to pick up the litter in my room, and she'd throw the trash away. If I did my task and she didn't, my mom knew exactly who to hold accountable.

You should be able to handle small tasks without adult supervision. You can do simple things like tidy your room, water the flowers, or pick up litter from the floor. Good tweens help with little tasks at home. When you do them, you're being responsible.

My mom would never allow me to watch my favorite cartoons until I had done my homework. She didn't do this to treat me badly. Instead, she was trying to teach me how to be accountable.

You can suggest to your parents some tasks that you can handle. Then, write them out in a book and check them off as you go. This will make you feel good and encourage you to get better at doing tasks.

Here's a checklist I used when I was younger.

Task	Yes	No
Sweep the kitchen floor		✓
Do the dishes		
Pick litter up off the floor		
Empty the trash can		
Load the dishwasher		
Water the flowers		
Feed the pet		
Get my bag ready for school tomorrow		
Do my homework		
Make my bed		

Discuss a time when you were accountable for your actions and didn't put the blame on someone else.

_____

_____

_____

_____

_____

_____

_____

Think Critically and Solve Problems

Can you tell your left hand from your right hand? If you can, then you're no longer a baby. Don't wait for someone to do everything for you. You can think for yourself and make certain decisions.

Making decisions and problem-solving every day can be difficult. Don't be scared; nobody was born with problem-solving skills. Even grownups sometimes struggle with critical thinking and problem-solving. This is why you should start learning now.

Critical thinking is learning from the experiences you go through every day. It helps you solve problems more easily. You'll also resist peer pressure and trust your judgment when faced with doing something you don't want to.

You can learn to think critically by:

Playing games

Your brain can become very active when you play games. In games, you face difficult levels, but somehow you still find a way to win and move on to the next level. Playing games such as a puzzle or chess, which require you to think deeply, can help develop critical thinking. It encourages your brain to adjust to new levels of difficulty and still find a way out of them.

Ask questions

Questions are very powerful. You learn by asking questions. If you don't understand something, ask someone who knows.

Brainstorm

Brainstorming helps you think about what reactions your actions might cause; this helps you choose rightly. Think about the different results that could come from a decision you want to make. For example, *"If I go to bed early tonight, what would happen? I'd wake up early for school, and I'll also be very active in class."* This is how you brainstorm.

Study how your parents make decisions

Learn from your parents. Study how they make decisions and what they consider before taking action. Then, listen to their suggestions and understand why they made their choices.

Join clubs

Joining clubs can help you experience life from a different view. You meet people and learn new things, making you think deeply about solutions whenever you face problems.

Exercise: Match these riddles in the left column to their answers in the right column!

Riddles	Answers
I am full of holes, but I hold water.	Eggs
I'm tall when I'm young but short when I'm old.	Matchstick
What building has the most stories?	Cold
I go up and never come down.	Mushroom
I am a room with no doors or windows.	Needle
I have keys but no locks.	Age
You must break me before you use me.	Sponge
I kiss my mother before I die.	Pencil
I have an eye, but I can't see.	Library
You can catch me, but you can't throw me.	Piano

Build Self-Esteem and Self-Confidence

Being a kid doesn't mean you can escape intense emotions. One minute, you're happy; the next, you're sad. I can relate to this. I remember questioning my worth and asking if there was anything special about me. I used to see other kids doing wonderful things and enjoying life. And there I was, doing chores at home.

You must have felt this way before. You thought that there was nothing special about you. You even felt like you weren't smart or beautiful enough. You got so sad and didn't want to do anything but sulk. If you think about yourself this way, you're harming your self-esteem and confidence.

How do you feel about your skills and talents? Do you think they're good enough? Self-esteem is what you think about yourself. It entails being in love with yourself—the way you think, walk, and talk.

With good self-esteem, you'll be confident in yourself, take on new challenges, try new things, and be open to learning new things.

On the other hand, self-confidence means believing that you can do anything, no matter how challenging it seems. You trust yourself to get through any situation. You dare to take risks and pursue your goals even after making a mistake.

Your self-esteem and self-confidence are like plants. If you water them regularly, they'll grow into beautiful flowers. But they'll dry up and die if you don't care for them. If you're constantly being harsh or talking down on yourself, you're harming your self-esteem and self-confidence.

You can build your self-esteem and self-confidence by doing the following:

Don't compare

You can't have the same things as your friends, so stop comparing! There'll always be that kid with what you want, and the kid probably wants what you have. But we can't all be the same; there's beauty in our differences. You're okay the way you are. You don't need to have what another person has to be your most beautiful self.

Be with people that make you happy

Who you spend time with can determine how you feel about yourself. So, run away from a friend who always makes you feel bad about yourself! You don't need them in your life. You need people that'll make you feel good when you do great things, correct you when you do badly, and encourage you to do better.

Be good to yourself

Only you can treat yourself the way you deserve to be treated. So, don't wait for anyone to encourage you. Do it yourself!

Every day, tell yourself how beautiful you are and how you're growing into an amazing kid. Start the day with affirmations like the ones below.

Exercise: Affirmations

Say these affirmations every day!

I am awesome	I am smart
I am special	I am beautiful
I am amazing	I believe in myself
I can do anything I want to do	I am kind
I will be great	I will have a great day
I have all that I need	I stand up for myself
I learn from my mistakes	I am determined
I refuse to quit	I am surrounded by love
My life is beautiful	I can do it, and I will

Write any other affirmations that come to your mind here!

_____

_____

_____

_____

_____

_____

_____

Develop Empathy for People

Empathy is your ability to understand another person's feelings, even when you are not going through the same problem. When you have empathy, you put yourself in someone else's shoes so that you can understand their pain and see things from their perspective.

To get along with people easily, you must have empathy. With empathy, you'll be more aware of how your actions affect others, what steps to take to be a good friend, and how to understand the people around you.

Let's assume that your best friend lost her cat. She feels sad and starts to cry. How would that make you feel? Sad, right? Why do you feel sad even when it wasn't you that lost your cat? It's because you have empathy.

Every day, people experience things that could make them feel sad. Empathy is what helps you to connect with them and feel their pain.

Whether at school, home, or the playground, you need empathy to make and keep friends.

Exercise: Find out how empathetic you are by taking the quiz below.

I...	Yes	No
Care about how other people feel		
Check up on others to be sure they're doing fine		
Consider how my words will affect others		
Try to help those who need it		
Find it difficult to say no		
Often feel sad when I see others sad or in pain		
Have people come to me for advice		
Don't interrupt when people speak		
Try to understand people's views even if I don't agree with them		

You can build empathy if you:

Be curious

Be curious to know what happens in the lives of people around you. This doesn't mean snooping around things that have nothing to do with you. Rather, it means showing concern when someone looks sad or does something out of the ordinary.

Listen

Most times, we aren't listening when people talk to us. We only hear the words come out of people's mouths. When a friend is speaking to you, forget every other thing and focus on what your friend is saying to help you understand them better.

Don't judge

It's easy to assume that people are wrong and deserve what they're facing because they caused it. This shouldn't be. For example, your friend broke her pencil because she was hitting her desk with it. Don't blame her for playing with the pencil. Instead, put yourself in her shoes and imagine how you'd feel if you broke your pencil too.

Exercise: Things I can do to show empathy to other people

Ex. Listen carefully when others speak

_____

_____

_____

_____

_____

_____

_____

_____

Safe Swimming

Physical activity is important for your health at this stage of your life. You need to exercise to strengthen your muscles and stay fit, and swimming is a great way to keep fit while having fun. It helps you burn unwanted fat, build strength, and put your mind at ease.

If you're looking for a fun way to cool off during the weekend, consider taking swimming lessons. Swimming is a life skill that comes in handy during emergencies. Nobody hopes for something bad to happen, but imagine if a situation requires you to swim. What would you do? How would you get to safety if you couldn't swim?

Here are a few things you should consider when learning how to swim.

Go with an adult
Going to the pool alone is too risky. You must always go with an adult to guide and help when you need it. Ensure the lifeguards are around before testing your skills and ask questions whenever you have concerns.

Don't swim alone
Having the water all to yourself is lovely, but it's more fun when you have friends to splash water on. Go with friends so that you can look out for each other in case anything goes wrong.

Don't play risky games with friends underwater
Stay away from games that involve pushing and hitting each other when you're swimming. Also, don't run around the pool. You risk getting yourself wounded because the surfaces

surrounding the pool are wet and slippery. Also, don't try to see who can hold their breath longer underwater—that can lead to drowning.

Go in with your feet first

Before you dive into the water, check for any sign showing the depth of the pool. If it's too shallow, stay away. If it's too deep for you, put on a life vest and swim close to the pool's edge.

Don't go near pool drains

Tell an adult to show you where the pool drain is and stay away from it. It could hook your hair or clothes and leave you struggling to break free underwater.

Don't jump in the pool to save a friend

If your friend seems to be drowning, look for a lifeguard or any adult around to help out. Jumping in the pool to save a friend is putting yourself at risk too. So, stay out of the pool and look for help.

Search for instructions

Always look for any signs before you dive into the water. Diving is prohibited in some swimming pools but permitted in others. So, if the swimming pool rules allow you to dive in, look around to be sure no one is already in the water where you want to go in.

Exercise: Search for the following swimming terms in the puzzle

Dive, Grip, Float, Swim, Kicking, Holds, Water, Bubble, Swimsuit

B	U	B	B	L	E	D	T
R	Q	V	D	G	R	I	P
W	A	T	E	R	U	V	Z
F	G	S	N	S	M	E	X
G	P	W	M	H	K	T	E
H	K	I	C	K	I	N	G
B	W	M	F	L	O	A	T
S	U	J	H	O	L	D	S

CHAPTER 5
GOAL-SETTING

Goal-setting is a skill that every human needs at each stage of life. As a tween, when trying to discover yourself and know what you love, you must learn to set good goals. If you want to become someone that knows what they want and goes for it, then you need to learn how to set goals. When goals are clearly defined, they have a way of pulling you toward achieving them.

Goals are what you want to achieve. They make you feel happy and satisfied when you get them done. As a kid, you must learn how to set goals for yourself. It's important so you don't get distracted by the many options you have to choose from.

I had an issue with speaking in public when I was younger. I would get nervous and blank out. I had to tell myself the truth; I needed to learn how to face the crowd and speak. I wrote things on a sticky note and placed it by my bedside so I could see it daily.

My dad paid for me to get into a public speaking class. I had to go there every weekend. On those days, he would tell me to take a deep breath after our meal so that I could make a sample presentation before the entire family.

At first, I didn't like the process. I didn't like that my weekend had been taken away from me. I wanted to play baseball during the weekend as the other boys did. But I also wanted to be great at public speaking. So I had set a goal and wasn't going to neglect it.

Goals keep you disciplined on days when you feel tired and just want to give up. With results in mind, you'll focus more and get it done. I put my all into learning public speaking; as expected, I got really good at addressing people.

The goal-setting skill I learned was useful for me. It was easy for me to improve my grades and other aspects of my life by setting the right goal. Goal-setting is the best way to create a happy future for yourself. Know what you want and focus on getting it done.

Identify Your Skills and Goals

You can't be setting goals if you don't know what you're capable of doing. You have to know your skills and then set goals. Your skills are what you can do right now. They can include drawing, writing, painting, and many other talents. Your goals are those things you wish to do now and in the future.

Now, ask yourself these questions: What are the things I can do? What do I want to do now or in the future? Write down the answers. This is the first step in identifying your skills and goals.

Exercise: Five things I can do easily

I can...	So I want to...
Ex. Paint	Display artwork at art exhibitions

Make sure your goals are things you really want to do. If your goals make you happy, getting them done will be easier. However, if they don't interest you, you'll be grumpy and reluctant to try them out.

Identifying your goals helps you feel confident. You'll also feel motivated to achieve your goals at all costs.

Many kids don't know how to identify their goals. You're still young and probably don't know what you're capable of. So discuss it with your parents. Ask them questions, and they will guide you.

When I discovered I loved musical instruments, I told my dad I wanted to learn to play the guitar. He smiled and told me that I could do it. And yes, with his encouragement and my determination, I did it!

There are many ways that your parents can help you identify your skills and goals. They could ask you what you want to be in life. They'll explain the cost of what you want to do and ensure that it won't overwhelm you.

Exercise: Some things I wish I could do are...

Ex. Play handball

_____

_____

_____

_____

_____

_____

I would be the happiest kid on earth if I could...

Ex. Play the piano

_____

_____

_____

If you've identified many goals, that's nice too! However, focus on one goal at a time. Once you've achieved that goal, you can move on to another one.

Doing too many things at once can overwhelm you. You might feel confused, lose focus, and barely get your work done. Prioritizing is a good way to choose which goal to work on first. It keeps you in check and ensures you're actually getting things done.

Learn how to prioritize

When you get home from school, you have two choices. You can decide to either do your homework or watch your favorite TV program. A good kid knows which one they should do first. Doing your homework first means that you've prioritized it over watching TV.

Prioritizing means placing things in order of importance. You need to understand that some things must come before others. For example, getting good grades in school is more important than playing games at home. You shouldn't waste your time by prioritizing unimportant things.

When you prioritize well, you'll manage your time and focus on your goals more. Emphasize the things you must do over the things you should do. There's a difference. Things you must do include your homework, reading, chores, and personal hygiene, among others. Things you should do include watching movies, games, and many others.

To prioritize well, you can decide to do all your class assignments or school projects on Friday. Then, you can relax and watch movies on Saturday. Your assignments come first because it's one of the things you must do. So, prioritize things that'll lead you to your goals.

How to prioritize

The best way to prioritize is to know what's most important to you. Then it will be easier to decide what to do first.

In the exercise below, write down what you should do and what you must do. You can also write down the things you wish you could do. Think about the consequences if you don't finish them. How terrible will the consequences be?

For example, you must do all your class assignments. If you don't, you will likely fail. Your teacher may report you to mom or dad, and they'll be upset with you.

I must...	I should...	I wish I could...
Ex. Do my homework	Take a stroll	Play baseball with my friends

The second step is finding the most and least important things. The most important things are those you must do first. Then, if there's any other task you want to do after that, let it come next.

If your most important task is completing your homework, do it first. Let the less important goals follow.

Write out all the tasks you need to do and rate them on a scale of 1-5 [5 for the most important and 1 for the least important]

Ex. I have to do my homework

_____

_____

_____

_____

_____

_____

_____

_____

The next step is to write how you plan to achieve these goals. A step-by-step plan will help keep you on track and point out mistakes you might make along the way. For example, if my goal is to buy a toy by the end of the month, my checklist would look like this.

- Save $3 every week
- Clean up the kitchen to get a tip from mom
- Drink water instead of buying soda

Having a plan like this will keep you focused and make your goals look achievable. Start with the hardest task on the list. The hardest task is usually the one that takes a lot of time to do. Doing this first will not only make you happier, but it'll also help you reach other goals easily.

The skill of prioritizing isn't inborn. However, you need time and constant practice to get used to it. This skill will groom you to become a responsible adult.

Sign Up for Programs That Support Your Goals

I knew I'd eventually become a writer. In my early years, I'd constantly write short stories and poems and show them to my parents. My dad would take his time to go through them and pat me on the back after reading them. Then, he'd smile at my drawings and encourage me to show him more of my stories.

I was unsure of what I was doing, but I continued doing it anyway. Then, when I understood myself more, I decided to join the "press" club in school. I was the youngest in the group at that time.

Joining the Press Club sharpened my writing skills. It made me feel more responsible, as I had to write stories to keep my peers interested in our school's notice board. The Press Club also exposed me to better styles of writing.

When you create a goal, you must also work your way toward achieving the goal. You can sign up for programs that support your goal. In my case, becoming a writer was my goal, and joining the Press Club provided me with the perfect opportunity to kickstart my writing adventure. Your goals decide which groups you join. If you want to be a baseball player, you shouldn't strive to be on the volleyball team.

Ask yourself this: "*What programs or groups are in line with my goals?*" If you can answer that question, proceed to sign up for such programs.

If you don't have an answer right away, don't fret. It might be because you don't understand how it works yet. You have your parents to guide you—tell them about your goals. Since they're more experienced, they'll provide the guidance you need to choose support groups wisely.

Exercise: Who I want to be

I want to be...	I should join...
Ex. A baseball player	The baseball team

There are many benefits to joining support groups. They include:

An opportunity to learn

Support groups help you to explore freely all you need to know about your goal. You can learn from the experience of different people there. You'll also find out which path makes your goal easier to achieve.

A network of people pursuing similar goals

One factor that makes your goals more achievable is having a network of people with similar goals. This ensures your goal is within reach. In addition, having these people around you is important for your self-esteem. Sometimes, you'll get sad because you aren't reaching your target. People who share your goals will encourage and guide you back on track.

Increased clarity

Clarity means a better understanding of your goals and how they can be reached. It's normal to be unsure sometimes of what your goal is. However, having a support group will instill the spirit of consistency. These programs will provide you with all the information you need to pursue and reach your goals.

CHAPTER 6
EMERGENCY SITUATIONS

Emergencies could happen when you play with friends or at home. They could be caused by mistakes such as a meal overcooked in the microwave or a gas leak at home. Natural disasters like floods or earthquakes could also cause an emergency.

I remember once when my cousin and his family visited during the holidays, we had gathered some wood and burned it so we could all sit around a fire and keep warm. We were playfully chasing each other around the burning pieces of wood when I accidentally stepped on a sharp stone. I didn't know it was serious until it hurt so much I couldn't place my foot on the ground.

I fell to the ground and cried for help. Both our parents had gone on a stroll some minutes earlier, so no adult was around. My cousin needed to act right away! He came over to where I was and helped me back to the living room. Then, he bent over to look at the wound. He poured water on the wound to rinse off the blood and applied iodine to the wound. I screamed because it hurt so much, but he applied it anyway. What my cousin did was apply first aid.

Emergencies can happen to anyone, whether young or old. This is why you should be prepared for anything. It would be best if you learned about the items in the first aid box and their uses. You might not be able to save the situation totally, but with first aid tips, you may improve the outcome.

First aid is what you do for someone experiencing a sudden sickness or injury, to ease the pain and stop further damage until proper medical care is available. A first aid kit is a box or bag containing items for treating minor wounds like burns, bruises, and sprains.

First aid saves lives

Lives are lost in emergencies every day. Yet, some of these lives could have been saved if the victim had gotten the proper first aid. Someone sick or injured might not be able to hang on until the arrival of health practitioners, especially if they're far from a hospital.

The simple first aid tips you know can make the pain bearable for the victim until they get professional help. Proper first aid can also speed up a person's recovery time and possibly determine whether they'll suffer a short or long-term injury. You'll also learn how to maintain your composure in emergencies.

First aid makes the professional's work easier

If you can provide first aid, the health practitioner wouldn't need to start from scratch to tend to the injured person.

First aid could also make communication with medical personnel easier. Since you were there to provide first aid, you'll be able to explain the situation to the health practitioner.

First aid is very helpful in cases where the victim can't move or speak.

First aid helps people feel confident

Kids who learn to administer first aid are respected by their family and friends. It'll also make a person feel more confident because they know they can treat themselves in an emergency.

They're more alert and focused and take precautions to ensure they're not exposed to mishaps or injury. Other people feel at peace when they have the first-aider to help them during an emergency.

What to Do During an Accident

You can't predict when an emergency will happen. If you could, it wouldn't be an emergency anymore. But we can learn what to do when an accident happens. This way, we'll be able to stay safe during an emergency.

What you do when an accident happens is very important; it could go a long way in saving your life or the lives of the victims. However, it's important to consider your safety before offering help in an emergency. It wouldn't be wise to risk getting hurt yourself when rushing to help an accident victim.

Here are tips to help you after an accident.

Don't panic

Asking you not to panic when an accident happens is like telling you to break down a locked door—it's hard, but not impossible.

Panic causes fear and shock, so try to understand the situation before making your move. Maintain your composure and don't panic. You'll be able to reason clearly and make sensible decisions when you're calm. Pause, breathe deeply, and carefully and logically assess the situation before moving in.

Use your first-aid skills

You're not too young to learn about first aid kits. Knowing about offering first aid helps you stay in control during accidents.

Know what the nature of the accident is. Is it fire? A bruise or a cut? Then, open your first-aid box and apply your knowledge to provide help to the person in need of it.

Call for help

As you approach the scene, look around to see if it's safe for you to help. If it isn't, stay away and call for help. You could dial an emergency helpline number on your phone or call your parents for help. Take all necessary precautions to keep others safe too.

Never put yourself in danger. It would be terrible if you ended up as another victim.

Exercise: Let's play "I spy" for first-aid boxes

I spy with my little eye...

Soft and white	Scissors
Liquid, transparent, and cold when applied to the skin	Plaster
Thin, transparent fabric	Gloves
Brown and sticky	Iodine
Used to cut things off	Cotton wool
I can wear it on my hands	Gauze

In the exercise below, write down what you think you should do when there's an emergency.

I should...	Yes	No
Make lots of noise when there's an emergency		
Handle an injured person with care		
Jump into the water to save someone that's drowning		
Call for adults or rescue services		
Check to see if it's safe for me to help		
Jump into a burning building to save my toys		
Check if an injured person is bleeding		
Use pressure to stop bleeding		
Administer any medicine I find in the first-aid box to the victim		
Wash my hands before touching the victim		
Touch the victim's blood with my bare hands		
Hide in my room when the fire alarm goes off		
Pour steamy, hot water on wounded areas		

Know the Basics of First Aid

Knowing how to use first aid could save the life of a loved one during an emergency. For example, if my cousin hadn't known about first aid, I would have been in terrible pain until my parents returned.

First aid is taught in schools to train tweens to care for themselves and their loved ones in emergencies. Therefore, be attentive whenever you're being taught the basics of first aid in your school.

You can also learn from your parents. Ask questions like "What can I do when my friend is sick?" or "What do I do when a fire breaks out in my school?"

You can also learn from your parents when they give first aid to people around you. Please take note of the things they do when you fall sick, the questions they ask you, and how they administer first aid before getting professional help.

There are some common things you should know about first aid.

Understand the situation

Always assess the situation before you administer first aid. Make sure it's safe for you and the victim. Don't just jump in to provide first aid right away.

Check the victim out. Is he suffocating? Is he unconscious? Is he in pain? How severe is this pain? What's his temperature?

Try to understand what's happening.

Exercise: A guide to assessing emergencies

Questions	Yes/ No
Can the victim speak?	
Is the victim unconscious?	
Are there any harmful things around—for example, knives and naked wires?	
Is the victim bleeding?	
Is the victim breathing?	
Can you feel the pulse points?	

Take common precautions

Common precautions you need to take while providing first aid include using disposable hand gloves, washing your hands, and covering your wounds and cuts.

These precautions are useful in most accidents. It is important to avoid spreading germs or complicating the victim's situation.

Exercise: Match the first aid remedies in the left column to the emergencies in the right column.

If someone is ...	
Choking	Roll them to the side and tip their head back
Has a bleeding nose	Apply cold, running water or a cold towel
Has a bleeding wound	Apply an ice pack
Has a broken bone	Apply an ice pack
Is in a fire	Drape a blanket over the person
Isn't breathing	Pinch the nose for ten minutes
Has a swollen injury	Apply pressure to the wound
Is in shock	Hit their back
Has a burn	Keep it still and support it
Has bruises	Call the fire department

Understand the use of first-aid kits

The first aid kit contains a lot of equipment. You can find gloves, bandages, scissors, plasters, pain relievers, and many other useful items.

A first-aid kit is important for every home to have on hand. You must know where it's kept in your house. Then, ask your parents or health teachers about using each item you find in the first-aid kit.

Exercise: Find the items in the first-aid box.

Plaster, Wipes, Gauze, Scissors, Bandage, Iodine, Water, Glove, Splint

M	Q	S	P	L	I	N	T
R	X	G	L	R	P	J	H
Z	C	E	A	D	I	T	A
S	C	I	S	S	O	R	S
F	W	D	T	Q	D	J	G
W	I	P	E	S	I	L	L
J	B	T	R	F	N	H	O
U	Z	W	A	T	E	R	V
K	G	A	U	Z	E	V	E

What to Do During a Fire, Accident, or Natural Disaster

No matter how careful we are, accidents are bound to happen in the home. It could be a fall or a serious fire. Fire emergencies and natural disasters are the most common types of calamities at home. You have to be prepared at all times.

Some tips to help you stay safe during a fire or natural disaster are:

Alert everyone at home

You might have a fire burning in a part of your house—alert everyone! It's the first safety step during a fire or a natural disaster. Shout loudly and ensure that everyone at home hears you. Shout "Fire!" and run out immediately. Don't wait to take anything with you.

Leave the building quickly

Don't try to hide in a cupboard or shelf to protect yourself, as you'll suffocate. Instead, find an escape route and run!

There's always an emergency escape route in buildings. You must ask your parents ahead of time where the one in your house is so you can bear that in mind in an emergency.

Don't go back into the building to save your toys. If your clothes catch fire, don't run. The fire will only burn harder if you run. Instead, lie down on the ground and cover your face. Roll around and around until the flames die out.

Use the back door if the main exit is blocked by smoke. Never open doors that feel warm. A door that feels warm indicates that there's already a fire in the next room. So, avoid going in.

If you must go through the smoke, bend low and find your way to your exit. If the smoke or fire has blocked your exit route, remain in the room and call the fire department. Wave a piece of bright-colored cloth through the window.

Call the fire and rescue service

If you manage to get outside, call the fire and rescue service. They are trained to help people who have had accidents. If you don't know their emergency helpline, you can ask your neighbors or grownups ahead of time.

When you call the fire and rescue service, you'll need to relax, explain the situation, and tell them your address. Your address must be accurate so they can locate you quickly.

CHAPTER 7
KNOW YOUR CORE VALUES

The term "core values" is more than just words. Core values are beliefs and behaviors that make up who we are as individuals. This means that every tween must be conscious of their core values if they aim to be responsible adults. If I believe that treating others well is important, that's my core value.

Core values aren't the same as your goals or plans; they go beyond that. If your core values change, your life and decisions change too. This is why finding and following your core values is essential. When you know and obey them, you have something to hold on to even when everything else around you is changing.

To identify your core values, be sure of the following:

What is important to you?

Your core values lie in whatever you strongly believe in. You naturally care more about them than any other thing. They push you to get up in the morning, and they keep you going— they are what gives meaning and purpose to you.

Look inward and think deeply. Find out those things that are important to you—the things you value over every other thing. These are your core values. You find yourself naturally abiding by them without anyone forcing you to. They are the things that every other aspect of your life is built upon.

Exercise: Write out some things you strongly believe.

Ex. I believe that God exists

_____

_____

_____

_____

_____

_____

What makes you feel good about yourself?

When you know your core values, you'll realize that your decision-making process will be more straightforward. This is because you have a foundation to guide you. You already know what you can accept and what you can't.

Your core values make you feel excited and satisfied when you live by them. For example, if I asked you "What behavior do you love the most?" what would your answer be? Whatever your answer is, it's one of your core values.

My core values make me feel good about myself. They're things I do regularly and without fail. And as long as I'm doing them, I feel good about myself.

Exercise: I get happy when...

Ex. I help someone in need

_____

_____

_____

_____

_____

_____

_____

_____

What goals make you feel proud?

I've accomplished many goals in my life. My favorite ones are in line with my core values. For example, I've learned to be patient and kind to others, even when they don't deserve it. I've also learned that it's okay not to know everything and ask for help when needed. I've learned the value of hard work because if I work hard enough at something, eventually I'll succeed.

All these have formed my core values. I'm in my best mood when I'm kind to someone. I also feel fulfilled when I achieve something I've worked hard for.

You can know your core values by thinking about what goals make you feel satisfied and fulfilled when you achieve them.

Exercise: I feel fulfilled when...

Ex. I tell the truth despite the consequences

_____

_____

_____

_____

_____

_____

_____

_____

What do others say is your best attribute?

If three of my friends were asked to describe me, they would probably say I am honest. This is because I hate telling lies. Honesty is one of my core values.

If people around you can't tell what your core values are, then you're probably not being true to yourself. You must be able to act out your core values. Let others see what you really stand for.

Here's an exercise to discover what your core values are.

Ask five people to describe your personality and write what they have to say.

Mom	•
	•
	•
	•
Dad	•
	•
	•
	•

Brother or Sister	•
	•
	•
	•
Friend	•
	•
	•
	•
Classmate	•
	•
	•
	•

When you know your core values, you're sure of which goals to focus on. You'll also relate with your friends better because they'll respect you for who you are.

Act Mindfully

Your tween years are a time of curiosity. You want to explore your environment and do new things every day. You want to jump and play and be excited about your birthday the next day. There's a lot to take in!

Do you take your time to be conscious of what's happening today? About how beautiful your walking steps are and how softly your mom speaks?

Mindfulness means being present in the moment. It involves thinking about what's happening now inside and outside of you—your feelings and thoughts.

Practicing mindfulness is easy; you just pay attention to what's happening right now. You can practice it anywhere—while waiting for the bus, walking by the road, or doing your homework.

You can sit quietly with your eyes closed, walk around the block, or listen to music. It's about being present in your life and becoming more aware of how each moment unfolds for you.

Follow these tips, and they'll help you stay mindful throughout the day.

Get enough sleep
You go to school, attend classes, play sports, do your assignments, and take extra or private tutorials. You start feeling like you don't have enough hours in the day to make all these happen. When you finally decide to rest, you still don't get enough sleep at night.

You'll wake up cranky, tired, and stressed. There's no way you can be mindful on a day like this. Getting a good night's sleep will keep you focused during the day. You'll also have more energy for whatever task comes your way. It's a perfect way to start being mindful.

Be kind to yourself

It's easy to get preoccupied with life and lose track of what matters most. You start forgetting how much you should love yourself, how funny you are, or how cute your smile is. It's never too late to change your mindset and behavior.

Check yourself out in the mirror every morning and notice how you stand. See how lovely your smile is and how long your hair has grown. Say sweet things to yourself.

When you're kind and loving to yourself, others will respond by being kind toward you too.

Pay attention to others

Being mindful of others can help you have a stronger bond with your friends. When you're conscious of others, you'll notice when they're upset or uncomfortable. You'll also understand how your actions affect others.

When you pay attention to others, you'll be more empathetic. This is because you know how others feel and what they need.

You'll find questions in the exercise below. Ensure you provide the right answers. The aim of this exercise is to increase your mindfulness.

Three things I can see now	• • •
How many lines are on my palms?	

What shape is my face?	
How many teeth do I have?	
Is the weather hot or cold?	
Is the sun out?	
Three things I love about myself	• • •
How many times does my heart beat in a minute?	
Watch how you smile in the mirror and write how it makes you feel	

Learn to Give Generously

Giving is a way for you to express your love for others. You're not too young to give. You can show love and give things out even as a tween. It can be as simple as buying your friend a snack or lending him your pencil.

You can change someone's life by giving them something they would really love to have. It doesn't matter how big or small your gift is; what matters is that it's appreciated by the person receiving it. Small acts of kindness can lift the spirits of others who are having a terrible day, and that can make you feel good too.

Giving is something you can do whether you're rich or poor. For example, if you decide to visit your friend's home, you're giving your time and presence.

Giving is a way to share your happiness. It's an act of love and kindness. When you give, you are expressing gratitude for the blessings in your life.

Exercise: Tick the list as you get it done

Stick a "good day" message on a stranger's car	
Give unused or lightly used clothes and toys to charity	
Pay your friend a visit	
Volunteer to rake the dried leaves off the grass	
Call someone you haven't spoken to in a while	
Pick up litter around the house	

Leave a tip for the cashier	
Take extra pencils and erasers to school and give them out	
Save up some money and give it to charity	

Learn Assertiveness

Assertiveness is not about being aggressive or challenging others. It involves more positive behaviors such as asking for help, expressing your feelings honestly and respectfully, standing up for yourself, and making choices that feel right to you.

Assertiveness is linked to confidence and self-esteem. So, a tween that is assertive is very confident. If you want to be assertive, then:

Be Confident

If you're afraid of being wrong, you'll never be assertive. Stand by what you believe in through thick and thin.

When you feel confident and know what you want, it's much easier to say it out loud. And when you say it out loud, other people will hear it and respond appropriately. If they don't respond appropriately, that's their problem—not yours!

Be Polite

If anyone does something you don't like, politely express how you feel to them. Be respectful when you call anyone out on their behavior. Keep your tone calm and polite. Be clear about what you are saying and why you think they should change their behavior.

Being polite doesn't mean that you have to agree with everything someone says or do everything they want. It does mean that you treat other people with respect, kindness, and empathy.

There are several ways you can be polite:

- You can say "please" and "thank you."

- You can ask for permission before touching someone else's property.

- You can wait for your turn when using a phone or other electronic device.

You may make mistakes at first, but you'll find that it's not impossible to be assertive. You'll gradually stand up for your rights and respect others too.

Exercise: Write X for assertive actions and Y for actions that aren't

Bossing people around	
Asking for help when you need it	
Being too shy to say how you feel	
Speaking against something wrong	
Shouting in public	
Leading a group of people to do the right thing	

Dealing with Rejection

Rejection is an unavoidable part of being human. We all experience it at one point in our lives. Let's say you want a cupcake, but your mom insists you can't have one until tomorrow. That's rejection. She refused to give you what you wanted. How do you feel about it? Sad, right? Regardless of how good you think you are, you can't run away from rejection. You can't always have what you want. Rejection is always hidden somewhere, waiting to strike.

There are ways to help you deal with rejection gracefully. They are:

Accept that rejection is a part of life

You'll fall into self-doubt if you react to rejection by feeling bad about yourself. You'll think you're worthless, and you'll become more desperate for approval.

So, just accept that rejection is a part of life. It happens to everyone, including me. We can't always get what we want and can't please everyone. So, it's okay if someone doesn't like something we do.

You can't change how others feel

When I was young, I thought everyone was like me. I had friends with matching interests, hobbies, and personalities. But this isn't always the case.

The world is full of different people. As you get older, you will realize how different others are from you. Everyone is entitled to feel however they want. So, it's not your duty to change a person's opinion. Let it be!

It's okay to be sad

It's impossible for you to always be happy. Times will definitely come when you won't be happy. Whenever you feel sad, just know it's a normal and constant part of life. It isn't a bad thing to experience sadness.

You may be disappointed with your performance at school, or your parents may deprive you of something you love. Situations like this won't make you happy.

You should learn to deal with sad moments when they arise. You'll definitely overcome them.

Talk to someone about it

A perfect way to deal with rejection is to pour out your mind to someone you trust. Once you do this, you make your heart lighter, and you feel better.

You could speak to a close friend or a family member. Talk to them about it and watch yourself get over the rejection more easily than expected.

Exercise: When someone tells me "no":

I will...	I will not...
Ex. Accept it and not feel bad	Ex. Overreact

Dealing with Strong Emotions

Emotions are what make us human. We can feel happiness or pain because we have feelings in us. These help us understand ourselves and connect with others better.

Too often, we ignore these feelings and bury them in the back of our minds, hoping they'll go away someday. But they don't. They stay in our minds and pile up. Then, they show their full strength when they're triggered. They become strong emotions.

Strong emotions are basic human feelings like anger, fear, anxiety, surprise, disgust, happiness, and sadness. They're an inevitable part of life. There's no need to be afraid or ashamed of them. The more you understand your emotions, the more you'll be able to deal with them effectively.

You can deal with strong emotions by:

Identifying your triggers
Why do you feel that way? Think deeply about what caused you to feel the way you do. Once you've done this, you will be able to watch out for what sets you off next time. This puts you in control of how you react to issues. You'll find out your next reaction won't be as bad as the first.

Putting a name to what you feel
If you push your feelings away and ignore them, they'll come back stronger. Instead, try to understand how you feel right now. It's not always easy, but it can help.

Identify exactly what you feel. If you're angry, say it. If you're scared, say that too. Calling the emotion by its name will help you relax and act wisely.

Talking it out

If you feel really down, talking the problem out can help. It doesn't have to be an organized conversation. Let it out anyhow it comes, get whatever it is off your chest, and move on. Discuss your feelings with a close family member or a friend about your concerns. You'll definitely feel better.

Identifying safe zones or tranquil activities

My younger sister was a lot of trouble for me. She often made me go against my parents' rules, so I kept getting in trouble. Guess what I did. Whenever I became upset with her, I'd pour a cup of water into my mouth and keep it there until I calmed down. It's funny, but it helped me to avoid fights a lot.

Finding an activity to distract you is best when you feel your emotions rising. Find something safe and put all your energy into it. It could be cleaning or humming. When you're settled, you can come back to identify what's caused you to feel upset and how to avoid it in the future.

For example, if someone has hurtful things to say about others, don't respond by attacking them. Instead, stay in a quiet place without distractions. Think about all that went down and respond calmly.

If someone criticizes your behavior or appearance in public, don't let them get under your skin. Just leave after saying something such as, "I'm sorry, but I have things I need to do right now."

Exercise: When I feel my emotions taking hold of me, I'll...

Ex. Silently count to ten in my head

_____

_____

_____

_____

_____

_____

_____

_____

_____

_____

_____

FINAL WORDS

Well done, buddy! You've finally reached the end of this book. Thank you for staying with me to this point.

When you were 6 or 7, you developed the foundation of your personality, which would, in turn, enhance your positive traits. By this time, you should be fairly independent and survive on your own around the house without calling for mom and dad's attention at all times.

Wouldn't it feel good if you could take charge and take care of things like the laundry, cooking, housecleaning, addressing a crowd, saving money, budgeting, and learning to be proactive in getting help when things turn sour?

Developing life skills is important so you can know what you want to do in life. It's high time you also begin to focus on keeping yourself informed on the things they don't teach you at school.

This book has discussed 25+ essential skills. With these life skills, you should be well-equipped to tackle the many hurdles you will face in life, and you'll know you can always turn to your parents for help at any time.

Don't read this book and assume that's all there is to it! To see results, you must read, practice what you have learned, and always refer to it when you feel stuck.

Good luck!

A FREE GIFT TO OUR READERS

For being our valued reader, we are offering you 4 books absolutely FREE today.

What You'll Get:

1. **11 Essential Life Skills** Every Teen Needs to Learn Before Leaving Home

2. How to **Be A Calm Parent** Even When Your Teens Drive You Crazy

3. 15 Tips to **Build Self-Esteem and Confidence** in Teen Boys & Girls

4. **Anxiety Help** for Teenagers

Scan the below QR code to download now.

Alternatively, you can visit:
www.thementorbucket.com/gift-bsls

MORE RECOMMENDED BOOKS

SELF-LOVE FOR TEEN GIRLS

9 Steps to Transform Your Mindset,
Build Self-Esteem, and Create a Life
You Truly Love

Get more details here:

www.thementorbucket.com/self-love

SELF-ESTEEM FOR TEENS

Mastering Self-Love and Building Limitless
Confidence (A Proven Path to Transform
Your Life and Achieve Your Dreams)

Get more details here:

www.thementorbucket.com/self-esteem

Want to Read More?

Before I close, I recommend you to read our other books in the series. These books are written especially for teens and their parents. You'll find them very helpful.

Get more details here:

www.thementorbucket.com/resources